Prentice-Hall
America's Role in World Affairs Series
Dankwart A. Rustow, Editor

RUPERT EMERSON
Africa and United States Policy

WALTER GOLDSTEIN
Military Strategy in World Politics

WILLIAM E. GRIFFITH
Cold War and Coexistence: Russia, China, and the United States

ERNST B. HAAS
The Web of Interdependence: The United States
and International Organizations

STANLEY HOFFMANN
Europe and United States Policy

CHARLES BURTON MARSHALL
The Burden of Decision: American Foreign Policy Since 1945

JOHN D. MONTGOMERY
Foreign Aid in International Politics

WILLIAM C. OLSON
The Making of United States Foreign Policy

DANKWART A. RUSTOW
The New Setting of World Politics

KALMAN H. SILVERT
Latin America and United States Policy

WAYNE A. WILCOX
Asia and United States Policy

JOHN D. MONTGOMERY
Harvard University

Foreign Aid in International Politics

PRENTICE-HALL, INC., ENGLEWOOD CLIFFS, N. J.

Library of Congress Catalog Card No.: 67-10171

Current Printing (last number):
10   9   8   7   6   5   4   3   2   1

C-32529 (C)
C-32528 (P)

PRENTICE-HALL INTERNATIONAL, INC.   London
PRENTICE-HALL OF AUSTRALIA, PTY. LTD.   Sydney
PRENTICE-HALL OF CANADA, LTD.   Toronto
PRENTICE-HALL OF INDIA (PRIVATE) LTD.   New Delhi
PRENTICE-HALL OF JAPAN, INC.   Tokyo

America's Role in World Affairs Series

Specialized knowledge and practical experience combine to lay the solid foundations for this survey of AMERICA'S ROLE IN WORLD AFFAIRS. Eleven distinguished authors distill their insights, refined in years spent as responsible government officials, as high-level advisers to governments, in prolonged field research, and in teaching at our leading universities. Their volumes emphasize the lasting realities underlying current conflict, the political forces in the present that will shape the world of the future. Separately, each volume in the series is a concise, authoritative analysis of a problem area of major significance. Taken as a whole, the series gives a broader and more diversified coverage than would be possible in a single book on American foreign policy and international relations.

An introductory volume by the series editor appraises the rapidly changing environment of foreign policy in the second half of the twentieth century—the revolution of modernization, the multiplication of sovereign states, and the tightening network of communication around the globe. In bold and deft strokes, William C. Olson analyses the forces of public opinion, congressional action, and planning and implementation in the executive branch that combine to shape American foreign policy. Charles Burton Marshall takes the reader to the inner councils of United States policy as he retraces with wit, urbanity, and a lively sense of drama some of the crucial turning points in our foreign relations.

Three volumes deal systematically with some of the major instruments of contemporary foreign policy. Walter Goldstein cogently links the breathless pace of military technology in a nuclear age to some of the perennial dimensions of human conflict and strategic calculation. The wide range of uses—the possibilities and limitations—of foreign aid yield to John D. Montgomery's penetrating treatment. Ernst B. Haas combines sober realism with a passionate sense of human interdependence in his succinct account of the contemporary pattern of international organization.

Another group of volumes takes us to regions where the drama of modern international politics is being enacted. The intimate and yet often frustrating relations between the United States and Western Europe are sharply illuminated by Stanley Hoffmann's irony and subtle understanding. William E. Griffith clarifies the awesome issues of Cold War and coexistence in the triangular relations among the United States, the Soviet Union, and Communist China. Wayne A. Wilcox, in a synthesis of rare breadth and depth, allows the reader to grasp the full complexities of that geographic concept called Asia. The problems of new states, with their bitter memories of the colonial past and their ardent hopes for a better future, are presented with sympathy and skepticism in Rupert Emerson's volume on Africa. Kalman H. Silvert draws on two decades of travel and study and on his keen sense for the explosive issues of evolution vs. revolution as he sums up the record of our relations with Latin America.

The contributors have sought no consensus of policy preference and no narrow uniformity of scholarly method. They share a conviction that policy must operate within a context of circumstance that allows now a wider, now a narrower, choice of alternatives and that sound policy must be formulated from a thorough knowledge of that context. They hold that valid theory in the social sciences must rise upon solid empirical foundations. They also believe that clarity and conciseness do not detract from true scholarship but on the contrary, enhance it. Within such broad assumptions, each author has applied his specialized knowledge and his practical experience to one distinctive facet of AMERICA'S ROLE IN WORLD AFFAIRS.

DANKWART A. RUSTOW

Preface

Writing almost any book about U.S. foreign policy is an act of defiance. If the book attacks current policies, time may turn its bitterness to sour grapes. If it defends them, history may establish right on the opposite side. But anyone writing about foreign aid can be sure of one thing: no matter when his words are published, the program will be in trouble on the Hill; its wastefulness will be freshly documented somewhere in the world; and the politicians, the administrators, and various segments of the press will be evaluating it from mutually inconsistent points of view.

In the months that have elapsed since I began writing this book, it has become increasingly evident that the United States government has relaxed its fears of Soviet expansionism. This development, in turn, has reduced the appeal of "bipolarity" as the ultimate rationale for foreign aid. Americans are discovering, as the British did during the height of empire, that national commitments become increasingly remote from the immediate neighborhood as new responsibilities of world leadership become manifest.

During this period as well, the economist's approach to foreign policy has gained in authority and urgency. Many who had sought a humanitarian basis for foreign policy became greatly concerned over the deterioration of the U.S. balance of payments position, and they have searched economic theory for means of reducing the American commitment. And long-standing skeptics of the political values of foreign aid have exploited an increased receptivity to their concern over the inefficiencies characteristic of development administration. The American public, for its part, sated with arguments over the responsibilities of world leadership, is finding grounds for serious disillusionment with the results of popular sacrifices for remote causes.

Considerations like these have convinced me that another effort to examine the nature of the U.S. commitment to world leadership is in order, especially in its political dimensions. As the lengthy bibliography at the end of this book will attest, there is no shortage of serious efforts to examine short- and long-term economic implications of foreign aid. But the political context of these actions—in the immediate and distant future, and in their intent and their consequences—has still not been adequately considered. Brief as it is, this book is an effort toward that end. Many of the arguments may seem familiar to the point of banality, but I hope their larger dimensions will emerge at least in outline more clearly than they have before.

In trying to deal with general problems in specific terms, I have relied on my own observations and experience in selecting and arranging what seems most relevant and important from the millions of words and statistics others have gathered. I can make no claim to universal knowledge, having examined only about eighteen aid programs in depth and visited or studied another twenty-odd in other connections. This exposure may not represent an adequate sample of a program that has covered over 100 countries and territories in the past 25 years. I have also used government sources for specific data, and thus perhaps exposed myself to capture by the bureaucracy. One thing I did to try to protect the reader from my own biases was to ask some of my colleagues to read and criticize the manuscript. They have done so, in ample measure, and I have taken much of their advice. I am especially grateful to Milton J. Esman, University of Pittsburgh; Hubert S. Gibbs, Boston University (Chapter 5); Lester E. Gordon, Harvard University; Bartlett Harvey, Agency for International Development; Karl Mathiasen, The Brookings Institution; James T. McCrory, formerly of Agency for International Development, now of Department of Health, Education, and Welfare; William J. Newman, Boston University; and Dankwart A. Rustow, Columbia University.

JDM

Cambridge, Mass.

Contents

To my wife

Introduction

In a fit of despondency Henry Adams wrote his brother Brooks at the turn of the century: "the world will break its neck within five and twenty years; and good riddance. This country cannot possibly run it. I incline now to anti-imperialism, and very strongly to anti-militarism. I incline to let the machine smash, and see what pieces are worth saving afterwards. I incline to let England sink; to let Germany and Russia try to run the machine, and to stand on our own internal resources alone." [1] Like many Americans, he was suffering disillusion-ment with the aftermath of the Spanish-American War and other nine-teenth century expressions of Manifest Destiny. His advice to "let the machine smash" was repeated often after the two World Wars, and several times the United States even attempted to follow it. On each occasion the attempt had to be abandoned.

The reasons why the richest and most powerful nation could not afford to let the others smash are complex but compelling. But if Henry Adams was wrong in wanting to let the world smash, he was certainly right in another part of his warning: "this country cannot possibly run it." The foreign aid program has been a disappointment both to those who think we ought to let the world alone, and to those who think we ought to rebuild it.

[1] Henry Adams to Brooks Adams, Feb. 7, 1901, quoted in Robert Osgood, *Ideals and Self-interest in America's Foreign Relations* (Chicago: University of Chicago, 1953), p. 78.

1

Americans have never been satisfied to let things alone. One of their persistent—and least charming—qualities has been the national desire to tinker with the world, hoping to improve it without really changing it very much. Even if they fail conspicuously, the mood of disillusionment never lasts long enough to drive Americans out of the world altogether. Each failure to reach the Promised Land brings a determination to try harder the next time.

United States involvement in foreign affairs is more than a simple-minded impulse to tinker. External changes have accompanied the gradual increase of United States power and prosperity: even if this nation wanted to rely on the oceans and the British navy for protection, it could no longer do so in a world of air and missile power, nuclear weapons, instant communications, constant peripheral threats to security, and, of course, a greatly reduced British capacity to protect American interests.

Nor can American interests be defined in the traditional way. The amount and disposition of private United States investment overseas no longer circumscribe the nation's foreign interest. The world is in some ways a more threatening place than ever before, and even the remotest of threats are almost immediately visible across the Atlantic or the Pacific. Sometimes an alarm is heard before the threats develop; and sometimes it has to be ignored, because if any form of preventive action is taken, an even greater threat might follow. The American stake in remote parts of the world can thus be quickly converted to one of self-protection as the danger of escalation rises.

The economic interdependence of the United States and the rest of the world is easily demonstrated. Steel could not be produced in an autarchic America; nickel, bauxite, tungsten, and chromium must be imported, to say nothing of consumer items such as coffee and cocoa. And while it is true that there are vast undeveloped markets for manufactured goods in the United States itself, the national economy, including its agricultural sector, is geared to produce surpluses for export. The American economy is clearly international. But it is also becoming increasingly evident that the American political system cannot survive in isolation, especially when other systems are almost irrespressibly expansionist. Unrest anywhere in the world is a potential trigger to a great power confrontation. And it must be remembered that with or without A bombs, the United States has less than 6 per cent of the world's population.

American wealth affords the average citizen twenty-five or more times the material possessions of his counterpart in many underdeveloped countries, but his political economy is inextricably related to those of other nations. In spite of its long-standing political stability and high productivity, the United States has not been made immune to the virus of international civil war.

American national well-being thus clearly requires an active diplomatic involvement in the affairs of other countries, sometimes in ways that seem only indirectly related to our own self-interest. This fact has been denied, accepted, and even overindulged at various times in the national history. The expression of national impulses in international action is a very diffuse and obscure process, involving private and public attitudes, presidential and congressional actions, and the activities of thousands of individual citizens on and off the government's payroll. In the twentieth century, few diplomatic actions are casual, spontaneous reflections of the national character.

Even if the original impulses behind American policy were perfectly spontaneous, they would lose that quality in their manifestations overseas. If the policies are important, they have been fought over at home; and if they have not been fought over, the effect of spontaneity is in all likelihood diluted by subsequent audits and reviews. Most diplomacy recognizes the futility of trying to seem spontaneous, and is deliberately formal and impersonal and predictable.

Whatever result an impulse may have after the debates and reveiws are over, it is seldom expressed impulsively or in isolated acts. American diplomacy in any country must take account of time and space; it must have some *continuity* with the past and some regard for the future, and it must show some *consistency* with what is being done in other parts of the world. Thus it is difficult for the United States to increase, decrease, or halt aid to a country that is momentarily in or out of favor, even if the policy-makers in Congress and the administration should want to. Sudden switches in policy reflect, or produce, some kind of crisis.

If the individual acts of American diplomacy must be seen in larger terms, so must the reactions and responses of the other countries involved. As already suggested, diplomacy strives to be somewhat predictable in order to reduce the dangers of misunderstanding and miscalculation. This element of predictability is, in fact, the very essence of foreign policy. But in world politics, the unexpected is commonplace: the consequences of one's own actions are never fully known, to say nothing of those of others. If Americans are sometimes amazed by their own decisions—in Cuba, Vietnam, in the Dominican Republic—it is even more difficult for them to be certain of the decisions of other nations. Crisis decisions are the least predictable of all, even when, as is usually the case, they arise out of fairly routine miscalculations on one part or the other.

Academic discussions of foreign policy therefore tend to sound either abstract or anecdotal. The pages that follow, insofar as they are systematic, are a defiance of nature. They seek to be systematic where no system was intended. They impose categories after the fact, and they offer classification schemes that do injustice to almost any given situation. They cite examples that cannot be taken as general rules. The only consolation is that all studies of foreign policy expose themseves to similar charges. It is left to each participant in foreign affairs to sense nuances and seek generalities. Even the most careful diplomatists and historians can mislead themselves in their search for the general and the analogous.

An even more urgent danger presents itself to those who avoid history and seek only to understand the immediate. It is important not to be misled by deceptively concrete language or by similarities between national and individual behavior. Foreign aid is not a carrot or a stick: it is seldom a reward and almost never provides an adequate means of punishment. It will not produce gratitude for a very long time, and if it did, it would be only an embarrassment between nations. It could not affect every country in the same way, even if it were offered in a standard form (which it is not). Aid will not even benefit the same political elements or economic sectors in different countries; sometimes it will bring the greatest good to the smallest number in spite of contrary intentions. There are ways of minimizing its adverse effects, once we have decided what these are, and once the donors of aid, both bilateral and international, have found ways of improving the prospects of success—when those, too, have been defined.

Henry Adams' discouragement with an intransigent world may have been well advised. Indeed, new grounds for discouragement are being discovered every day. But it is now obvious that we are all mounted on the same fast-moving machine and it is important for us to develop better means of controlling its direction. No one ought to suggest that control is easy. Nor should one expect foreign aid to save mankind, though it is hard to see how one could argue that the world is worse off because of it (some do, however, as we shall see in Chapter 2).

Social problems of great complexity have been successfully attacked since World War II: depressions have been averted; and wars have been confined and limited. The fact that foreign aid may relieve some of the distress of poverty encourages the hope that it may also reduce the appeal of communism; the possibility that it may stimulate economic development suggests that it may give a restless intelligentsia a stake in peaceful change; wherever peasant farmers can see an advantage in offering their political loyalty and steadfastness, the work of the revolutionary and the guerrilla recruiter may become more difficult. The hope placed in foreign aid, when largely conceived, is essentially a hope for the future: that it is possible, for example, to "buy time" against the prospects of ultimate political disaster—the takeover by forces that cannot be displaced; and that by so doing, foreign aid can indirectly contribute to the possibility of a decent and peaceably changing world order. How best to use the time that is bought—in Vietnam, for example—has not yet been clearly answered. Foreign aid can sometimes influence the actions that governments undertake during the period of grace it has bought, but it is seldom used for that purpose. Time bought by foreign aid enabled Greece and Turkey to flourish and the Diem regime to survive for nearly a decade, but the initiatives for action lay with other governments; and foreign aid held European self-respect together long enough to permit the endogenous revival of nationalism and the exogenous rise of internationalism. Time did nothing for Indonesia, however, and in Burma it was no asset. The Philippines, too, were unable to fill the void left by the death of Magsaysay, though the years of leadership he did give would not have been possible without foreign aid.

Although foreign aid is addressed to the great issues, it is also used, often far more successfully, for small ones. Many great problems of the latter part of the twentieth century cannot be solved by foreign aid: how to counter subversion, for example; how to develop strong and responsible leadership in the underdeveloped countries; or how to balance the multiple threats of Peking and Moscow. This book will suggest uses to which foreign aid is being put in both large and small problems of world politics, and we shall explore its approaches, its tools, and its tactics. The chapters will also offer appraisal of its successes and failures and an estimate of its future.

Doubts and problems will remain even if larger questions of foreign aid should be satisfied over the next decade. But if the world machine remains out of any one nation's control, there will be few statesmen content to let it smash without making some effort to avert that catastrophe.

1

The Uses of Foreign Aid

No aspect of American foreign policy has consistently aroused more controversy than foreign aid. Every year, new laws have to be passed first to authorize the program and then to appropriate money for it. No fewer than ten committees and subcommittees in the two houses of Congress renew, challenge, and pass on foreign aid activities. The issues posed by foreign aid are profound, and feelings about it run deep.

Foreign aid as we now generally understand it began in the excitement of postwar European reconstruction under the Marshall Plan. Each phase that followed—Point Four, Mutual Security, and international economic development—involved a different rationale. The annual renewal of these programs introduced new legislative struggles and imposed an increasing burden upon the American Presidents who had to develop political support for them. Dwight D. Eisenhower described foreign aid as the least understood function of the government, and John F. Kennedy stated, half seriously, that he would gladly discontinue it if he could. But he found he could not; and it has survived review and criticism by both parties, changing administrations under four Presidents, and re-examination by every Congress since World War II. During this period it has been pressed into the service of nearly every major foreign policy and many domestic issues as well. Controversy has attended it at every turn; it has achieved few complete successes or unconditional failures; and its continuance remains an issue to be resolved anew every year.

Foreign aid has many different roles to play in American diplomacy. It serves to create or dramatize a symbolic national "presence" abroad; it is used in exchange for international favors; and most recently it has tried to introduce or influence changes in other countries. The first two of these purposes are related to traditional forms of international relations, although in both cases the doctrines and methods are distinct from historical diplomatic approaches. The third, however, is an innovation in international politics. Thus foreign aid is not a single, unified program, but a complex instrument of national policy and domestic politics. Its purposes are interlocking and sometimes contradictory. One distinguished diplomat has likened it to a screwdriver, because it has so many potential uses, both wise and foolish. Much of the controversy over its alleged successes and failures has arisen from a confusion about the purposes to which it has been put. Since most American foreign aid is intended to serve more than one purpose, evaluation is a subtle, not to say hazardous, task.

For the sake of convenience, three forms of aid may be distinguished according to their major purpose: Diplomatic, Compensatory, and Strategic.[1] Although many overseas aid programs contain all three of these elements, it is usually possible to identify these separate strands of foreign policy in the priorities and character of any country's program.

DIPLOMATIC FOREIGN AID

Since the heroic days of Benjamin Franklin, American diplomacy has often attempted to establish abroad a "presence" that suggests national ideals like generosity, humanitarianism, efficiency, technological excellence, and recently, sheer power. Often our major ambassadors have been larger-than-life Americans chosen to demonstrate qualities not related to conventional diplomacy at all; and the career foreign service officers who staff our embassies have also felt the urge

---

[1] Any classification of foreign aid operations is arbitrary. Some students may prefer Professor Morgenthau's categories (humanitarian foreign aid, subsistence aid, military aid, bribery, prestige, and economic development aid). Chester Bowles classifies aid in terms of countries (nations requesting aid because of maldistribution of wealth; nations with inadequate GNP, willing to mobilize their own resources; nations lacking the competence, organization, and will to use aid; and nations whose situation is unclear). The Agency for International Development (AID) is using a threefold schema like mine (development, security-stability, and limited objective). Purely economic categories have also been advanced, notably by the Center for International Studies at M.I.T. I prefer the classification suggested in this chapter, because it places the aid objectives of the United States in the context of its aspirations for a world order.

to reflect whatever version of the national ideal was ascendant, regard-gardless of their other duties. But the American presence includes, as well, the marines being landed to display or exercise power, the actual and imagined secret agents of the CIA and other intelligence agencies, and the casual and not-so-casual tourists, businessmen, and movies and kinescopes. Not all projections of the American image abroad are benevolent, controllable, or even predictable.

Congress found ways of symbolizing American humanitarianism abroad long before foreign aid was conceived. As early as 1812, for example, it voted funds to dispatch grain to Venezuela after an earthquake disaster; [2] and again in 1847 and 1880, the United States Government authorized the Navy to ship relief goods to Ireland.[3] Such gestures did not become automatic, however; in spite of the Venezuela precedent, Congress defeated proposals to authorize funds for direct aid to Greece in 1827, to Ireland in 1847, 1861, and 1880, to the persecuted Jews in Russia in 1892, and to the victims of an earthquake in Chile in 1939. No United States government-financed technical assistance mission abroad was authorized until one was organized for Liberia in 1909.[4] On the whole, humanitarian purposes have invoked private aid far more frequently than they have attracted public funds.

The use of diplomatic means to establish a national presence of the United States in other countries was greatly enlarged through the operation of programs of economic and military assistance following World War II. This form of presence has been used both to demonstrate official friendships and to influence the state of world politics. But international friendships change, as do national intentions. Diplomats are often hard pressed to reflect current national purposes, and many Americans have expressed concern over the impression created by their compatriots working in their embassies abroad.

The Official Presence: Diplomats and Overseas Staffs

The American presence abroad today requires the services of an official community of at least 65,000 employees. Of these, the Defense

---

[2] The appropriation was $50,000. 2 Stat. 730, May 8, 1812. E. Taylor Parks, "Foreign Aid—150 Years Ago," *Foreign Service Journal,* July, 1962, pp. 36-39, and in AID's *Front Lines,* Feb. 15, 1964, p. 4 and Feb. 28, 1964, p. 4.

[3] 9 Stat. 207, Mar. 3, 1847, and 21 Stat. 303, Feb. 25, 1880. Congress also authorized the use of naval vessels to transport private U.S. contributions to sufferers in the Franco-Prussian War. 16 Stat. 596, Feb. 10, 1871. Similar use of Navy transport was authorized for relief to India. 29 Stat. 701, Feb. 19, 1897.

[4] The proposal was first made in 1859. Congress appropriated $20,000 for it on Mar. 3, 1909, but it was not fully implemented. E. Taylor Parks, *Front Lines,* Mar. 13, 1961, p. 4; Merle Curti and Kendall Birr, *Prelude to Point Four: American Technical Missions Overseas 1838-1938* (Madison: University of Wisconsin, 1954), p. 66.

Department has by far the largest number, well over 35,000, not including the combat zones (compared with only 331 in 1938). The State Department, the Agency for International Development (AID), and the U.S. Information Service also have large cadres overseas, and smaller numbers are working for the departments of the Treasury, of Commerce, of Health, Education, and Welfare, and of Agriculture. At the end of 1963, about 5,000 technicians were serving abroad either on contract or as government employees. In 1964, over 10,000 were working in Peace Corps assignments in 46 countries.

The size of this group has alarmed many critics of United States foreign operations. In recent years, American policy has deliberately limited the size of embassy staffs and aid missions to offset the impression that swarms of Americans are infesting the world's capitals. In 1957, for example, after a visit to the Far East and Africa, Vice-President Nixon recommended reductions in the size of the American overseas staffs because of his concern over the resentments caused by their relatively high living standards (for few official Americans feel inclined to ask their families to sacrifice their health and comfort by "going native"). American leaders were also apprehensive when Yankee-go-home slogans and charges of neo-colonialism accused the United States of plans to take over the functions vacated by its imperialistic allies. In order to reduce their overseas staffs, however, the United States had to deny some countries' requests for badly needed technicians. At the time of the Vice-President's visit, the U. S. aid agency had been processing requests for 1,400 technicians in the Middle East and South Asia; but after the Vice-President's report, it reduced the authorized figure to 800. It was thus both an American "absence" and the American "presence" that conditioned the subsequent American image in this area, as these governments protested the reduction in their quotas of American technicians.

The American presence means different things to different people in countries where tourists and technicians are wanted but signs of affluence are resented.

The Unofficial Presence

In addition to the official American community abroad, there are some 30,000 American missionaries and 25,000 American citizens working overseas in business enterprises, making a total population, including dependent families, in the hundreds of thousands.[5] This form of American presence abroad (in addition to some millions of tourists each year) sometimes overshadows the impact of foreign aid efforts.

The activities of missionaries and voluntary service agencies both

[5] Harlan Cleveland, Gerald J. Mangone, and John Clarke Adams, *The Overseas Americans* (New York: McGraw-Hill, 1960), pp. 82, 104.

parallel and contrast with modern foreign aid. Many missionaries have offered educational and medical services along with their religious teachings, and even today much of the primary education available in Africa and elsewhere can be traced to European or American missionary origins. Especially under the influence of the Social Gospel movement of the late nineteenth century, missionaries felt a call to relieve human ignorance and suffering. Even those who conceived their role in purely doctrinal terms found their secular activities— especially teaching—useful in engaging the interest and loyalty of potential converts. And in countries such as Turkey, missionaries were tolerated as teachers and doctors only so long as they made no attempts to convert. The experiences of the missionaries have provided valuable insights into the nature of technical assistance.[6]

Institutionally, however, the activities of foreign aid are very different from those of private volunteers. The practice of foreign aid depends upon government-to-government relationships for its entry and authority, rather than upon those among private individuals. The isolated missionary can work as a kind of "Ugly American" if he chooses,[7] teaching and demonstrating better ways directly to peasants and farmers; while for diplomatic reasons, foreign aid technicians must usually work at one remove from the mass of the population, hoping to find ways of imparting their knowledge through government agencies that will in turn extend technical services to their own citizens. A sense of obligation to serve humanity may underlie both official foreign aid and private missionary activities, but the techniques appropriate to each are fundamentally different. Missionaries are not usually encouraged to work through government channels: they want to change individuals, not whole societies. By contrast, technical assistants on the payroll of a foreign government are not usually permitted to work as isolated individuals or to try to convert host nationals to a new way of life. Such an approach would violate well-established norms of international relations and offend the sensibilities of a sovereign government. No regime could permit employees or "agents" of a foreign power to work at will among its citizens.

The closest official approach to missionary technical assistance is that of the Peace Corps, which, in contrast to the Agency for International Development (the principal foreign aid agency), sends groups of workers to serve as if they were employees of the host country. For the Peace Corps technician now in Latin America, and

[6] Edwin A. Bock, *Fifty Years of Technical Assistance* (Chicago: Public Administration Clearing House, 1954); Curti and Burr, *Prelude to Point Four.*
[7] William J. Lederer and Eugene Burdick, in *The Ugly American* (New York: Norton, 1958), present a layman's view of the follies and potentials of foreign aid. A useful companion to this novel is Joseph Buttinger, "Fact and Fiction on Foreign Aid," *Dissent,* Summer, 1959.

Africa, and Asia, the experiences of the missionary as an individual teacher working in a strange culture are intensely relevant. It is possible that the Peace Corpsman has more in common with the missionary in terms of techniques and approaches than he has with the foreign aid technician.

The Peace Corps is the newest element in United States foreign assistance, but it, too, has historical precedent. In 1901, William Howard Taft sent the "Thomasites" as volunteer teachers to the newly occupied Philippine Islands.[8] Like the Peace Corpsmen of two generations later, they found that teaching in an underdeveloped country required personal qualities of bravery, ingenuity, and generosity. Some may have seemed paternalistic in spite of, or because of, their good intentions. But Peace Corpsmen are working in independent countries, not in colonies, and their relationship with host nationals can develop with relatively little mistrust of American motives. Observers in many countries have noted the good will generated by the activities of this handful of Americans working in projects far from the major cities. The Peace Corps offers foreign aid in its most personal form, but above all it is a demonstration of national presence and international idealism. Because of its size, it may not be of decisive economic value, but its energy and good will have made it the most exciting display of the American presence in many parts of the world.

Private Investment

Private American investments constitute both a national presence and an important source of economic development abroad. American investments create so large a force in some countries that they are the equivalent of a large scale aid program. As Table 1 shows, more than $30 billion are invested abroad by private Americans, over a third of which is dispersed among the underdeveloped countries. Some American firms abroad have established major educational and medical services for their employees and the surrounding community. The example of Firestone in Liberia is often cited as dramatic testimonial to private support of hospitals and schools that have generated opportunities unparalleled in other parts of the country. The "demonstration effects" of good management in the developing countries have also encouraged other industries to undertake similar economic development. In a dramatic reversal of the paternalism of foreign investors in the past, companies such as Sears, Roebuck in Mexico and

[8] Willis P. Porter, "American's First Peace Corps," *Saturday Review*, July 20, 1963, p. 45; Geronima T. Pecson and Maria Racelis, *Tales of the American Teachers in the Philippines* (Manilla: Carmelo and Bauermann, 1959). The "Thomasites" were named after the converted cattle cruiser that ferried them overseas.

Casa Grace in Peru are assisting local entrepreneurs to establish independent companies to provide housing and transportation and to develop "feeder industries." These activities often closely resemble foreign aid projects.

TABLE 1 • *DIRECT U.S. INVESTMENTS ABROAD*

Location	1950		1960	
	Millions	Per cent	Millions	Per cent
Canada	$3,579	30.37	$11,198	34.20
Europe	1,733	14.70	6,645	20.30
Latin American republics	4,445	37.70	8,365	25.55
Western Hemisphere dependencies	131	1.11	884	2.70
Africa	287	2.43	925	2.82
Asia	1,001	8.50	2,315	7.07
Oceania	256	2.17	994	3.03
Other international	356	3.02	1,418	4.33
Total	$11,788	100.00	$32,744	100.00

* Source: *Foreign Economic Policy, Hearings Before the Subcommittee in Foreign Economic Policy of the Joint Economic Committee,* U.S. Congress, Dec. 4-14, 1961 (GPO, 1962), p. 481.

Large-scale American business activities overseas sometimes stimulate local business ventures as well. Training programs, personnel practices, and purchases from local industry (especially those engaged in supplying and processing raw materials and in transportation) have improved the management and diversified the activities of the private sector abroad. In 15 years of contract service to the Ethiopian Airlines, TWA developed it to the point where 76 per cent of its employees were Ethiopian. The Philippine-American Life Insurance Company also made important contributions to economic development in the Philippines through accumulation and investment of private capital in housing and other building projects.[9] American

[9] The National Planning Association has prepared a series of case studies analyzing American business performance abroad. These include *Sears, Roebuck in Mexico,* May, 1953; *Casa Grace in Peru,* November, 1954; *The Philippine-American Life Insurance Co.,* March, 1955; *The Creole Petroleum Co. in Venezuela,* December, 1955; *The Firestone Operations in Liberia,* December, 1956; *Stanvac in Indonesia,* June, 1957; *The United Fruit Co. in Latin America,* June, 1958; *TWA's Services to Ethiopia,* April, 1959; *The General Electric Co. in Brazil,* January, 1961; *IBM in France,* April, 1961; and *Aluminium Ltd. in India,* January, 1962.

investments overseas, especially when undertaken by the large and more enlightened corporations, can make an important contribution to a positive national presence.

Not all American business activities abroad have improved the national image, however. Marginal commercial operations have also flourished on the periphery of large-scale economic and military assistance programs, weakening the impact of aid projects and discrediting the very institution of private capitalism. Stories of faulty engineering, shoddy goods, and exorbitant prices from American "privateers" can be heard in many capital cities in the underdeveloped world.

Apart from actual misconduct, the political preferences and activities of American business have not always coincided with those of the State Department. In Latin America especially, United States enterprise has been accused of supporting conditions of social stability at the expense of social justice, thus contributing to a political vacuum that has encouraged extremes of both left and right. Moreover, United States aid programs are accused of supporting projects beneficial to large companies but of marginal value to the mass of the population or general economic development. One observer noted that "banana republics" had been provided with roads leading to United Fruit and other large private holdings rather than to the undeveloped interior; that nearly all the large Latin American mines are owned by United States corporations (or were, before they were nationalized); and that United States aid loans go to American corporations rather than to deserving locals.[10] Similarly, when the United States decided to withdraw its support from a proposed consortium loan to Indonesia, it was said that the U.S. bilateral aid continued nevertheless in the hope that Indonesia would live up to its commitments to American oil companies there.[11] These specific charges are hard either to document or to disprove, since they deal with national motives. Roads to large industrial plantations, for example, are often the most economic investment, even though they may benefit an American corporation; and aid to Indonesia was generally thought of as a "presence" program rather than a support to private companies.

[10] John Gerassi, *The Great Fear: The Reconquest of Latin America for Latin Americans* (New York: Macmillan, 1963), parts V and VI. Other examples appear in Miguel Ydigoras Fuentes with Mario Rosenthal, *My War with Communism* Englewood Cliffs, N.J.: Prentice-Hall, 1963).

[11] *The New York Times*, Sept. 25, 1963. Aid has also been withheld from countries that seize American property. In 1963, a $3 million program for Ceylon was canceled because no agreement had been reached on compensation to U.S. oil companies for 63 gas stations taken over in 1962. In July, 1965, U.S. aid was resumed after the Prime Minister offered a $10.5 million settlement. There were reports that compensation of the oil companies would be covered by a loan from Britain (*The New York Times*, July 4, 1965).

The issue is an important one, however. The need to avoid accidentally enriching irresponsible commercial elements both in the United States and abroad has forced aid administrators to adopt cautious procedures and take time to investigate and reaffirm each step of project operations. Although aid is usually intended to benefit a country as a whole, specific aid projects are bound to benefit some citizens more than others. But when American aid enriches a group already privileged, whether legitimately or not, there is dissatisfaction. Even when the host government decides to use United States aid to benefit a preferred business community, the resulting scandals may create an unfavorable image of venaity that becomes vaguely associated with the American official presence. For many years, American aid administrators tried to avoid associating United States funds with private commercial elements abroad, thus leaving important decisions regarding the private community to the government. More recently the paradox has been resolved: United States aid administrators have found ways of enlisting the services of the private sector. They no longer rely so heavily upon public efforts to support economic development, while espousing the ideals of private enterprise. Aid continues, nevertheless, to expose itself to charges of benefiting further the sector that is already richest.

Diplomatic and Ceremonial Gestures

Establishing a favorable American presence abroad is a traditional diplomatic activity. Humanitarian gestures and ceremonial gifts offered through the ambassador have been occasions for a display of American national virtues. Some of them even encountered difficulties foreshadowing modern foreign aid. The 1812 Venezuelan earthquake relief appropriation mentioned on page 8 (under "Diplomatic Foreign Aid" and in footnote 2), for example, was a preview of later failures in administration: the shipment was seized and distributed through commercial markets to finance counter-revolutionaries. The United States gesture of friendship only contributed to defeat for the Venezuelan Republic and American hopes for it.

Ceremonial gifts have also been used in traditional diplomacy to create an impression or establish a national presence. Fabulous and exotic presents to and from Chinese emperors are matters of historical record as well as legend and fairy tale.[12] Ceremonial gifts are still presented by the United States to new heads of state, but in recent years these have taken the form of tractors instead of Cadillacs. Grain, universities, and roads may be offered by a new ambassador

---

[12] A history of foreign aid as used in traditional diplomatic interchanges of all kinds appears in George Liska, *The New Statecraft, Foreign Aid in American Foreign Policy* (Chicago: University of Chicago, 1960), Chap. II.

for purposes not unlike those prompting European and American offerings of weapons and model trains to the Japanese Mikado a few generations ago. In their modern form, such gifts still serve to display good will and esteem and to exhibit power, wealth, and an advanced technology; and they still serve to commemorate symbolic occasions such as coronations, the arrival of new ambassadors, anniversaries, and most recently, the achievement of independence. By 1963, the United States had spent over $795,000 for Independence Day gifts to 15 African nations, including a two-engine plane for President Felix Houphouët-Boigny of the Ivory Coast, mobile health and X-ray units for Sierra Leone, a health and educational film library for Cameroun, and 300 scholarships for the Congo.[13]

Today's fashion to offer useful economic gifts to newly independent nations has often led to public misunderstanding as they begin more and more to take on the appearance of economic aid. When foreign aid funds are used to support ceremonial scholarships and ceremonial building projects, the absence of support to more basic economic programs has become a reproach to foreign aid programming, even though for generations such gifts have been given without regard to economics or technology. These reproaches have been especially inconvenient when the aid agencies have had to improvise an otherwise nonexistent economic justification for such ceremonial projects. The use of foreign aid funds and personnel to make a favorable impression has diverted more than one American aid program from the long-range political and economic objectives for the recipient country.

Foreign aid was used more and more in the 1950's as a means of estabishing a national presence; but for the most part, such efforts did not depart significantly from traditional diplomacy. They were usually conceived in response to the desires of the government of the host country; but as the cost of establishing a national presence has risen in proportion to the gains, foreign aid programmers have begun to wonder why economically and technically sound projects could not serve the same purpose, and better. The fact is that Diplomatic foreign aid, although responsible for most of the popular criticisms of the program, represented a very small proportion of the total effort—certainly less than 10 per cent—by the mid-1960's.

COMPENSATORY FOREIGN AID

Not long ago, a member of the Nigerian delegation to the United Nations called the late American Ambassador Stevenson and com-

---

[13] *The New York Times,* Aug. 13, 1963.

plained that a member of the U.S. delegation had threatened to with-draw United States aid to Nigeria unless Nigeria voted in favor of a certain proposal. Stevenson immediately disavowed any such threat, the Nigerian vote was cast in accordance with previous instructions from Lagos, and the incident was closed. But in the minds of many observers of foreign aid, there remains the impression that it is a form of bribery and therefore an undignified way of conducting dip-lomatic relations. Similarly, the suspension of United States aid to Panama during the canal crisis of 1963 was erroneousy interpreted as a form of coercion, or bribery in reverse; the aid would be restored, it was assumed, as soon as the Panamanian diplomats acceded to the American terms. The fact that the aid had been offered originally as "conscience money"—the canal tolls really were inadequate as of 1963—would justify us in considering it Compensatory aid, even though administrative haggling rather than reverse bribery had caused the suspension.

International transactions of this sort are as old as the relation-ship of empire and tributary. During the Middle Ages, feudal loyalty and protection were regarded as the normal obligations of the weaker and stronger states, respectively, to each other. Giving tribute in exchange for a nonaggression pact was a form of self-defense; pay-ments by remote kingdoms in exchange for continued independence was at once a forerunner of gangsterland's "protection" and a treaty of alliance. A cynic could argue that in the new diplomacy the roles are simply reversed, with the stronger nations paying the weaker ones for favors.

Although not as complex as certain other political usages of foreign aid, international exchanges of favor are among the most delicate of diplomatic relationships. Gifts so given require reciproca-tion, often hard to achieve among nations and therefore a potential subject for recriminations. Even if the threatened withdrawal of aid to Nigeria and the actual suspension of aid to Panama were doubtful cases, equivalent threats are repeated in Congress every year when foreign aid appropriations are debated.

The commonest forms of these international exchanges involve the use of a military base, air rights, and adherence to alliances, all of which have been "purchased" with substantial economic or military assistance instead of cash payments.

The use of Spanish bases between 1953 and 1963 was approved in an agreement that coincided with Export-Import Bank loans amounting to $500 million during the ten-year period. When a new five-year agreement was arranged in September 1963, further bank loans of $100 million were offered over the next few years. All of these loans were to be earmarked for economic development purposes, and they thus bore some resemblance to United States foreign aid programs in the underdeveloped countries. Over the period 1949-1962, United States aid to Spain of all types totaled $1.695 billion, nearly three-quarters of which were in the form of grants, both military and economic. Elements of the program used for economic purposes included some important sums to industry and mining, transportation, food and agriculture, and other technical assistance and capital projects. These figures do not include approximately $500 million spent in Spain during the decade in constructing and operating the bases, which also made economic contributions to the nation.

Exchanges involving the use of overseas facilities for military bases create a dual American presence: first, that of the troops and technicians necessary to man and operate the base; second, the staff involved in administering "aid" projects of various kinds that are offered as compensation for the use of the base itself. In the first instance, of course, the American presence is associated with a military purpose usually transcending the strategic interests of the host country; in the second, the "aid" projects involved are often capricious in terms of the economic need of the country. Thus in neither case is the American presence part of a rational economic aid program, although there may be incidental benefits to both countries from the flow of servicemen's dollars and the operations of the secondary projects. Moreover, these activities are frequently a source of political embarrassment because they are undertaken out of considerations that seem alien to the general purposes served by the American presence elsewhere. Because these exchanges result in expenditures that are planned and administered by AID in the underdeveloped countries, they are often confused with them.

Some critics have argued for a return to direct compensation for the use of such bases as a way out of the embarrassment. Much criticism of foreign aid could no doubt have been avoided if Spain or Portugal has received rent for the military bases they had supplied, instead of forms of economic assistance that created the appearance of United States political support to dictators. But even if such cash agreements could have been negotiated, the resulting relationships would still present potential sources of international friction. The governments of Spain and Portugal do not want to sell or lease their territory, although they are quite open to international exchanges of favor. In any case, the value of a base or of continued adherence to an alliance would be difficult to assess in terms of rent; and however generous the rental figure, there would no longer be any expectation of having it used for developmental purposes.

It is unlikely that the use of foreign aid as a medium of exchange will be abandoned. Even in the case of Spain or Portugal, American officials have tried to use the aid on economically sound projects, causing improvements that might not have taken place if the cash equivalent of the United States aid had been turned over to the regimes in power. Some agreements, moreover, have to be negotiated quietly and with no visible purchase of favors. The foreign aid agencies must therefore continue to bear the stigma for such negotiated assistance and to rely on public sympathy and congressional understanding to protect their other operations from criticism that relates to international bargaining.

STRATEGIC FOREIGN AID

Foreign aid is more than an extension of the American presence or payments for international favors: it is a strategic reflection of a world outlook. This is its third and most novel use.

The most dramatic, and riskiest, of the American foreign aid operations have been those intended to improve the world order. The world order sought by American diplomacy is not simply one of dominance and dependence. It calls for a delicate network of constructive interrelationships. It involves support to diplomatic ventures by friendly nations, like the foreign aid Taiwan and Israel have offered in Africa, both of which were made possible by continued American capital and technical assistance. It also involves a concern for internal conditions likely to influence world politics, since the foreign aid doctrine assumes that United States foreign policy can serve American interests by helping other nations achieve what they legitimately want or need. This assumption of an identity or convergence of certain basic interests among the noncommunist nations rests on the proposition that all seek to maximize their sovereign independence and to improve the living standards of their people. When these conditions are not present, foreign aid usually retreats to a Diplomatic or Compensatory form and loses its strategic drive.

United States postwar diplomacy has assumed some responsibility for encouraging conditions favorable to a world order that will neither endanger the security of the United States nor threaten the elements contributing toward freedom in other countries. Economic development, technical modernization, and social and political reforms are bound up with this American commitment.

The range of instruments available to the United States in advancing such a world order includes *military action* to create strategic bastions against the military expansion of the communist world, as in South Korea; *military aid* to maintain the independence of other countries that are threatened by the spread of communism through insurgency, as in Laos and Thailand; and *economic aid* to encourage the development of forces that will improve internal conditions, as in Brazil and Nigeria. In some cases, American aims may be limited to gaining time for a political evolution that will produce a degree of stability (a concept to be examined in Chapters 3 and 4) and evidence of progress. In other parts of the world where subversion and insurgency are still more remote, American aid programs can be directed toward serving higher political ideals of the nations involved.

Each of these forms of diplomacy requires some involvement in the domestic affairs of other countries, however objectively the United States plays its role. Strengthening the military capabilities of countries threatened by border aggression often produces an internal disequilibrium among the political forces contending for domestic power. Thus Thailand, Pakistan, and Korea are examples of countries dominated by military forces that have benefited from American aid. Using foreign aid to promote stability in countries not threatened by direct aggression also introduces an element of political involvement. The reforms proposed by the Alliance for Progress to increase the prospect of success in the developing sectors have often been strongly resisted in Latin America. In Taiwan, too, the efforts of the Sino-American Joint Commission on Rural Reconstruction strongly influenced the political process. Even purely technical programs of modernization have contained social and cultural overtones and produced political repercussions: education often contributes to unrest, especially among unemployed intellectuals; new technical skills breed new classes, sometimes to the discomfort of the governing elite; improvements in agricultural technology have had an important impact on the family structure, especially when less skillful members are no longer needed for production; and as industries develop, so do cities, with their special social problems. The rationality involved in industrialization and modernization may produce secular attitudes disturbing to the religious traditionalists. It is no wonder that, important as they are, programs directed toward strategic goals of this order are politically the most difficult areas of foreign aid.

Foreign Aid and Neo-Colonialism

In some parts of the world, American foreign aid has been represented as subtle subversion or neo-colonialism, and critics have found ways of equating the purposes of the United States with those of the former imperial powers. The United States, indeed, did have a brief experience in colonialism in the Philippines, although it was marked by a unique determination to create conditions of eventual self-government. But the ultimate purposes of foreign aid have been to strengthen, not weaken, the capacity for self-determination. Still, the charge of neo-colonialism is an appealing way of focusing the politics of envy, the resentments of the exploited, and the preferences of the neutralists. And recent trends in United States foreign policy have given new life to the accusation.

The charge of neo-colonialism received unexpected support when, near the end of the 1950's, "Buy-American" strings were administratively tied to all foreign aid procurements. Instead of offering funds for use anywhere in the free world,[14] it now became necessary for the aid recipient to purchase goods and services from the United States wherever possible. Prior to 1958, the United States had insisted upon worldwide bidding for most aid procurements. It was concern over the loss of United States gold to other industrial countries that led the government to tie its aid so tightly to American producers. Many critics of United States foreign policy interpreted this requirement as a device for dumping high-priced or unsaleable American goods and creating a form of dependence on American industry, shipping, and commercial enterprise.

Charges against these forms of American mercantilism or economic colonialism were given additional impetus late in 1963, when both President Kennedy and AID Administrator David E. Bell attempted to gain public and congressional support for foreign aid by arguing that it increases American exports and opens up export markets for the future. The President cited the cases of Taiwan, Colombia, Israel, Iran, and Pakistan as examples of nations whose import patterns had been dramatically affected by foreign aid. "These used to be the exclusive market of European countries," Mr. Kennedy said. "Too little attention has been paid to the part which an early exposure to American goods, American skills, and American ways of doing things can play in forming the tastes and desires of newly emerging countries—or to the fact that, even when our aid ends, the desire and need for our products continue, and trade relations last far beyond the termination of our assistance." [15]

The President's argument was, of course, designed for domestic consumption. It was part of his campaign to restore the unprecedented budget cut that Congress had inflicted on the foreign aid program in the preceding weeks. Such domestic arguments were given wide publicity in the United States, though they were ignored by Congress (which seized the occasion of the 1963 foreign aid appropriation to make its largest budget cuts since the inception of the program). And if the argument was not successful in Congress, it was even less so overseas. In their concern over neo-colonialism, beneficiaries of

---

[14] Even before 1958, some aid goods (coal and certain agricultural commodities, for example) had to be supplied from U.S. sources, if possible, and Export-Import Bank loans were always tied to American procurements.

[15] *The New York Times*, Sept. 18, 1963.

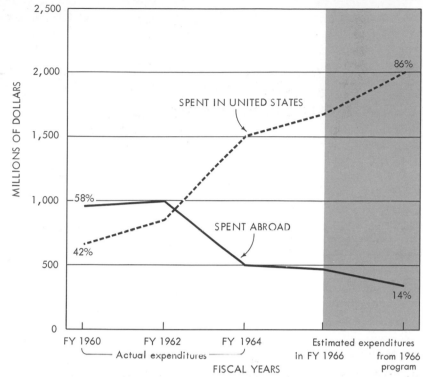

Source: Agency for International Development, *Front Lines* (July 15, 1965).

Where the AID money was spent

United States aid overlooked the fact that a larger proportion of United States aid money has been used on a worldwide procurement basis than the proportion of foreign aid offered by any other country.[16] But it is not difficult to find supporting charges of mercantilism, even though foreign aid programs have predominantly reflected strategic rather than commercial objectives. Recent legislation has been passed forbidding the use of aid to support projects that might yield exports competitive with United States products. As a result of such gestures, the nation seems to be becoming mercantilist in spite of itself.

The impurity of America's motives in offering foreign aid is taken for granted by its own citizens, accustomed as they are to associating baseness with nobility in many political processes at home. But the injection of domestic politics in a phase of foreign policy designed to serve major strategic purposes has undoubtedly weakened the Ameri-

[16] Nearly all European aid is tied to purchases in the donor country. The trend in that direction in the U.S. has been marked. Whereas only 41 per cent of U.S. aid was actually used for American goods in 1960, the figure had increased to 92 per cent by 1965. (AID, Operations Report as of June 30, 1965.)

can response to charges of neo-colonialism. It is true that foreign aid seeks, by strengthening other countries, to protect sovereignty rather than to destroy it. It is also true that the ultimate aim of strategic foreign aid is to promote economic growth and diversification in the developing countries rather than to create conditions of dependency on the United States. But as American economic and military power exerts itself in areas hitherto unaffected by U.S. influence, at least the appearance of dependence grows. Foreign aid tends to expand communications, to increase imports, and to enhance influence. No nation is truly autarchic, but weak nations are especially sensitive about their dependence, because the flow of influence is so strongly against them. If the United States is to use its power and influence for purposes it regards as necessary or good, it assumes an empire of obligations that it cannot decolonize.

The empire of obligations is an especially heavy burden when military aid is offered, even though it may be related more to the maintenance of sovereignty than to the establishment of an American hegemony on foreign soil. Most military aid, in fact, is carefully shielded against imperialistic ambitions. During the early 1950's, for example, 78 per cent of the $5 billion yearly U.S. Military Assistance program went to NATO; and even as late as 1962, two-thirds of a much smaller total was devoted to various international headquarters and multilateral programs. Large amounts went specifically to countries on the border of potential or active Communist aggression: Greece, Turkey, Korea, and Vietnam.[17] Forty-one other developing countries received only 3 per cent of the total, mostly for training, small arms, communications equipment, and civic action. Once again, however, the rationale offered at home for this aid tends to undermine the American posture of anti-imperialism abroad. It has been common to justify the military aid program by arguing that it supplies and equips 2.5 million troops at an average cost of one-tenth the salaries alone of the same number of Americans. To be sure, this justification rests on the strategic assumption that strong, independent, non-Communist countries will strengthen the free world, not that these troops are enlisted in the defense of the United States. But not all nations receiving U.S. military aid assume that free-world defense is synonymous with their requirements, as the 1965 war between Pakistan and India was to demonstrate.

Military aid has had some unfortunate consequences, though it has not created conditions resembling colonialism. Some countries

[17] These countries received, directly and indirectly, about half the U.S. military aid total. In the proposed 1967 program, almost three-fourths of the total will go to countries adjacent to USSR and China (Vietnam excluded).

receiving it became less, rather than more, dependent upon the United States for their own defense. An American military presence remains, however, the most dangerous form of strategic foreign aid, and the rationales offered for domestic consumption sometimes increase the risk of failure.

Contrast with Communist Foreign Aid Strategies

The distinctive characteristic of American aid is its strategic use in assisting other nations to attain economic, military, political, and social conditions that will contribute to a world order conceived to serve the ultimate interests of the free nations. It is the nature of this desired world order that distinguishes the American from the Communist approaches to foreign aid. Rivalries of technique, differences in style, and even contrasts in the national presence are subordinate to these differences in purpose.

For the United States, promoting a peaceful and just world order is a major aim of foreign policy, and foreign aid has been used since its inception in hope of minimizing causes of world tension (even though it contributes incidentally to dissatisfaction by encouraging the "revolution of rising expectations"). The USSR and especially China, on the other hand, have offered strategic aid in order to increase tension because fundamental change is essential to achieve the desired Communist world order. Because of their recent and dramatic emergence to the status of world powers, China and the USSR have been able to use economic aid to create a heroic mass impact and to generate admiration for Communist achievements. Like U.S. aid, Communist credits have promoted economic development and technical modernization; but the economic development of the non-Communist world, especially in the private sector, is not a primary objective of Sino-Soviet aid. For the Communists, revolution against capitalism everywhere remains a major goal, and they have not hesitated to use foreign aid to serve this political purpose. Political development in the direction of stronger governmental authority or of a "worker-state" represents a basic objective of the Chinese and Soviets. Their aid devotes special attention to finding ways to increase the scope of government enterprise, to support mass movements, and to encourage the industrialization of agricultural activity along Soviet lines. The U.S., on the other hand, acts on the assumption that some of the most serious threats to peace are economic and, therefore, concentrates its aid on developmental projects. In an ironic reversal of Marxist economic determinism, the Communists have concentrated on politics, and the capitalists on economics. The United

States has not devoted much attention to political development even though it considers trends toward democracy to be in its interests. In recent years, there has been a dawning American recognition of foreign aid's potential as a support to democratic institutions and social progress, but no doctrine of democratic development has emerged as a guide to U.S. action abroad.

The absence of an adequate political rationale in the American foreign aid doctrine is responsible for a deliberate policy of relying on technical and economic criteria in assessing its achievements, while China and, in the earlier days, the USSR, secure in the conviction that other considerations should be subordinate to politics, have seemed relatively unconcerned with technical and economic failures if political purposes were served.

Both blocs offer aid for traditional reasons and as a form of international bargaining, but only in the strategic uses of foreign aid as a diplomatic instrument do the distinctive elements in these two programs appear.

CONCLUSION

These three uses of foreign aid are distinct enough to permit classification of major projects in one category or the other. Most military aid, for example, is clearly a product of American international strategy, as are programs of economic modernization. Prestige projects, on the other hand, whether given to celebrate the inauguration of a government, to reinforce the credentials of a new ambassador, or to match a Soviet gift, are equally clear efforts to demonstrate a friendly American presence; hence they belong in the diplomatic category. And loans or projects negotiated in connection with a base rental or other specific favor should be classified as compensatory aid. Sometimes, of course, a single project represents a mixture of purposes.

Taken collectively, U.S. foreign aid in any one country represents an amalgam of impulses to establish a national presence, together with miscellaneous international bargains or exchanges of favors and various strategic purposes. Attempts to judge the program as a whole by any one of these criteria often suggest failure; some programs that have been celebrated for their dramatic technical impact or diplomatic success have, in fact, failed to achieve their prime objectives. Evaluation is possible only when aid projects are judged in terms of their primary purposes.

This obvious fact is not as simple as it seems. It is still possible for a single rationale—whether diplomatic, military, political, or economic—to smother the rest. In recent years, economic criteria have dominated official policy. Such considerations led to a decision to terminate aid to Taiwan in 1965.[18] The assumption that economic prosperity will assure desirable political developments is one that will be severely tested in Taiwan during the decade ahead, when its problems of political succession may cause the United States to regret a withdrawal dictated by purely economic consideration.

There are many reasons for offering aid, and a variety of ways of doing it. If the economic instruments of development are no longer needed, other instruments more suitable to U.S. strategic purposes can still be useful. The American government is only beginning to recognize this possibility.

[18] See Angus Maddison, *Foreign Skills and Technical Assistance in Economic Development* (Paris: Development Center of OECD, 1965), p. 14. A similar decision will remove foreign aid as a source of American influence in Greece and Israel.

2

The Instruments
of American Aid

No single proclamation or law created the foreign aid program. Foreign aid came as a series of creative responses to specific challenges, after the United States government had discovered the constructive potential of using its economic resources abroad. The strategies for such uses were conceived separately for each country and region in crisis, in accordance with the degree and nature of United States' interests. Each decision was taken piecemeal and in the midst of searching debate. There was no Grand Design: some strategies became clear only after the crises had been resolved. And the choice of means only gradually came to resemble tactical doctrine.

The first decisions came during and immediately after World War II, when the United States was still very unsure of its role as a peacetime leader but was conscious of its unprecedented power. The invention of the atom bomb had introduced to some observers new conceptions of American military leadership, while to others its deterrent power suggested the possibility of a return to isolationism as the nation demobilized and began to withdraw its troops. But even before the Cold War had ended the hope of disarmament, the United States found itself forced to re-engage in world affairs. The new strategies were economic, but the tactical uses took many forms.

The resources that were transferred through these first experiments in foreign aid are now roughly classified as "capital" and "human." Usually both forms of aid are necessary in the underdeveloped countries, in order to achieve important and self-perpetuating social or institutional innovations. But in Europe, no such extensive commitments were required. Historically, the first form of postwar foreign aid was therefore the direct transfer of capital, since the skills and the institutional organizations needed for the rebuilding of Europe were already at hand. In the years following the European reconstruction, aid was extended to Asia and Africa, where human and institutional capabilities were in short supply. In these areas, programs of technical assistance for the development of human resources had to supplement, and sometimes precede, the transfer of capital.

Developing human resources in an institutional context required new approaches to aid. Person-to-person technical assistance was too heavily dependent on isolated individuals to achieve the massive, sustained impact needed. Foreign aid strategists also discovered that their efforts could be lost unless joined by a deliberate, conscious program of support to the "nation-building" or political aspect of development. Each of these approaches to aid developed its own rationale, but limitations of both knowledge and will continued to hamper the creation of an integrated theory of foreign aid.

In spite of the extensive findings of economists and other social scientists, foreign aid has remained an art rather than a science. The instruments of aid are still used in different combinations according to the best current judgments of ambassadors, economists, field technicians, administrators in Washington and abroad, and interested congressmen.

CAPITAL AID: THE NEW DOLLAR DIPLOMACY

Dollar Dimensions

In the first 20 years after World War II, the dimensions of foreign aid were reckoned at $116 billion. This is the sum obligated in a variety of ways to some 120 aid-receiving countries (see Table 2). Actually only $67.248 billion was spent for Foreign Assistance Act [1] programs, but this sum remained far more than any other nation had even spent abroad in peacetime, and the fact that over 70 per cent of it was for economic purposes made it all the more impressive.

The United States had extended aid to friendly nations at much

[1] The Agency for International Development and its predecessor programs, together with the Military Assistance Program, obligated $72.939 billion during this period, of which it actually spent $67.248 billion. The remaining $6 billion was in the "pipeline," that is, assigned to projects (often large-scale construction such as hydroelectric dams and power supplies) that had not been completed by 1965. Funds used to set up development banks and credit agencies are also considered in the pipeline until the funds are paid out to these institutions.

faster rates in the two World Wars, to be sure. Loans to the Allied
Powers in World War I amounted to a net loss of $7 billion for the
United States, and there was an additional $3.1 billion in postarmistice

TABLE 2 • OBLIGATIONS AND LOAN AUTHORIZATIONS IN U.S. AID

Fiscal years 1946-1965 *

Region	Military	Economic	Total
Near East & So. Asia	$ 6.3	$17.3	$23.6
Latin America	.9	9.4	10.4
Far East	9.9	16.2	26.1
Africa	.2	3.1	3.3
Europe	16.2	30.5	46.7
Oceania and Canada	.1	.2	.3
Nonregional	1.0	4.7	5.7
Total	$34.6	$81.4	116.1

* In billions of U.S. dollars. Includes UNRRA, Export-Import Bank long-
term lending, Food for Peace, and a large number of miscellaneous programs. Source: U.S. Agency for International Development. All figures in
this table are rounded, and therefore do not necessarily add to make the
totals supplied.

loans for relief and reconstruction.[2] And American assistance in World
War II, largely through lend-lease, amounted to $40.93 billion.[3] But
these sums represented a national defense effort, which, in times of war,
has never been niggardly.

Aftermath of World War I

Outlays for wartime purposes did not create a new doctrine of
fiscal involvement abroad in the 1920's. After World War I, the United
States refused to experiment with foreign aid even when important purposes were involved. In 1923, for example, Secretary of State Hughes
specifically denied that the United States government had any responsibility for supplying food or raw materials or for rebuilding war-dam-

[2] William Adams Brown, Jr. and Redvers Opie, *American Foreign Assistance*
(Washington: Brookings, 1953), pp. 2, 3. This figure excludes payments of principal and interest on these loans of about $2.8 billion. Private lending for military
and reconstruction purposes before and after World War I totaled $11 billion;
and although not all of the principal was repaid, the interest payments and portions
of the principal repaid totaled a net gain. (*U.S. News & World Report*, XX, No.
21, May 17, 1946, p. 11.)
[3] Thirty-eight countries received this aid, most going to Britain, Australia,
New Zealand, South Africa, India, France, and Soviet Union. The total grants
were $48.1 billion, and additional credits amounted to $.97 billion. Repayments,
including reverse lend-lease, return of ships, cash settlements, and repaid loans,
totaled $8.17 billion. At the end of the war, lend-lease aid that was already in
the pipeline for delivery was used for the transition to peace. This amounted to
$6.7 billion in net grants and $8.6 billion in net loans. (*Ibid.*, pp. 82, 116.)

Foreign Assistance Act expenditures as a per cent of U.S. gross national product

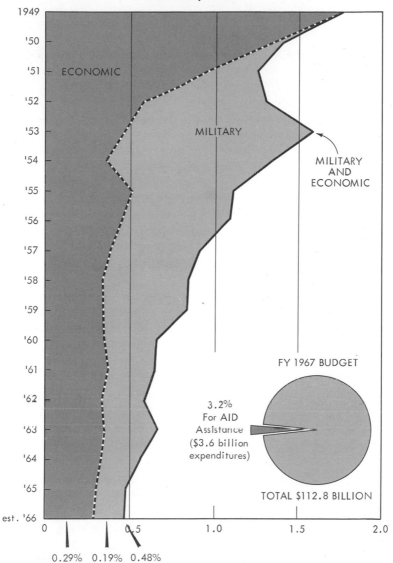

PER CENT

aged Europe or restoring its money and banking systems. "It is not the policy of our government to make loans to other governments," he observed in August of that year. Again, in 1927, Secretary of Commerce Herbert Hoover stated: "If nations would do away with the lending of money for the balancing of the budget, for purposes of military equipment or war, or even that type of public works which did not bring some direct or indirect return, a great number of blessings would follow to the entire world." Both the purposes and the methods of foreign aid as now conceived were repudiated.[4]

These views not only prevented the use of official American credit for diplomatic purposes, but they also led to attempts to cut off private loans for European reconstruction, for fear the result would be a contribution to rearmament. In order to reduce the commercial attractiveness of European ventures, the United States government required its allies to give priority to repaying war debts before amortizing private loans. Mr. Hoover specifically warned potential investors that the United States would attempt to collect on defaulted war debts at the expense of private loans. A few years later, Secretary of State Hughes suggested that the government officially discourage or even prohibit loans to governments where the United States would have difficulty protecting foreign investments.

But in the end, the denial of private credit to Europe was a diplomatic failure for the United States. Early efforts to control commercial loans proved unsuccessful because private interests were convinced that Europe was a good risk. In 1922, President Harding, concerned that private credit was being used against United States interests, wrote his Secretary of State, suggesting that he request private bankers not to lend to countries that were preparing to increase their arms expenditures. But restricting private loans in order to encourage disarmament—an important American goal—proved unfeasible. Even when commercial loans were not made specifically for the purchase of armaments, they indirectly served that purpose. When national budgets in Europe were balanced with the aid of private American loans, purchases of military equipment were financed indirectly by simple transfer of funds from one account to another. Private United States loans to Germany and other countries thus helped rearm Europe in spite of the government's intentions. The policy of relying on (and trying to control) private loans for basic United States diplomatic purposes was a twofold failure: the government could not effectively prevent the use of private capital

---

[4] Herbert Feis, *The Diplomacy of the Dollar* (Baltimore: Johns Hopkins University, 1953), pp. 5-18, discusses the significance of these changes in American policy.

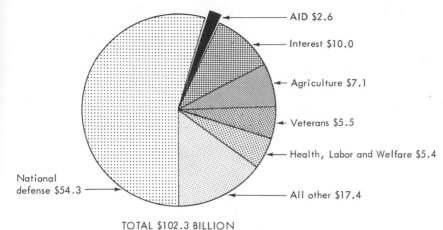

TOTAL $102.3 BILLION

AID'S share as per cent of the federal budget, FY 1963—new obligational authority, in billions of dollars

for purposes it disapproved, and the policy itself prevented the United States government from extending public credit for purposes that it favored.[5]

It took another war, with its even more severe tasks of reconstruction, to produce the policy of using public capital for diplomatic purposes. In departing from the view that an impropriety was involved in government funding of foreign projects, United States policy discovered a variety of reasons why capital assistance should be rendered to friendly countries.

[5] There are some exceptions to this statement. It is possible that denying private credit to some countries that had defaulted on their war debts may have assisted in the collection of these debts. France, Belgium, Italy, Greece, Romania, and Yugoslavia were all denied direct loans from either public or private enterprise until they had made satisfactory arrangements with the U.S. Treasury (although there was some evasion because short-term credits were extended by banks and other companies with American affiliates). Other positive diplomatic achievements during the period included advice to the Latin American republics on financial and other measures that would increase their credit ratings, a policy that may have been incidentally beneficial to the U.S. economy. On the other hand, the failure of the U.S. government to restrain loans to support Japanese expansion in China far offset these gains, and it is also possible that unrestricted loans to Germany during the Weimar period increased the overextension of German indebtedness and thus may have weakened the capacity of German democracy to withstand the economic pressures that contributed to Hitler's rise. During the interregnum between the World Wars, there was some use of American credit to reconstruct the physical facilities and economic systems of Europe, and private funds also made it possible for the Germans to pay reparations and for the Allies to repay war debts. But private credit during the Depression years did not serve American diplomatic purposes well, especially in Japan, Italy, and Germany.

The Issue of Controls

Once capital has been transferred to other hands, its path is hard to follow, much less control. Since World War II, capital assistance has taken a variety of forms, from outright dollar grants to support a foreign currency, to less-than-cost sales of military equipment or agricultural commodities and guarantees to World Bank capitalization. Whatever its form, the United States government has exerted itself to prevent waste and misuse. That is why, except in cases of emergency, the United States does not normally give grants for general budgetary support or to make up the deficits of other countries. Even emergency relief operations are carefully audited.

The difficulty of controlling the end use of funds by the United Nations Relief and Rehabilitation Administration (UNRRA) led to the first great congressional challenge to the principle of peacetime foreign aid. As an international organization, UNRRA had begun by late 1945 to resist American suggestions regarding distribution of its funds, most of which came from the United States. Washington insisted on establishing priorities based on need rather than on diplomatic negotiation, and it objected to some projects altogether.[6] By August, 1946, the issue of controls doomed UNRRA: the United States Congress was not willing to support grants to countries that might use them for purposes of which it did not approve. Grants involving "untied" dollars would thereafter be administered only where necessary and on a bilateral, government-to-government basis, with administrative authority to discontinue support to objectionable or wasteful activities.

The issue of control over foreign aid dollars was still not resolved, however. Even issuing grants bilaterally did not guarantee the United States a veto over projects they might indirectly make possible. Often when a governmnt wanted aid money to carry on a luxury or political project of which the United States disapproved, it asked for funds to support an important and unchallengeable project and then diverted equivalent amounts of "its own" funds to the marginal activity in question. This was not necessarily a strategy designed to deceive American taxpayers; often it was merely an attempt on the part of the aid user to harmonize his own set of priorities with those of the United States.

---

[6] In the first year, Congress authorized a U.S. contribution of $1.35 billion of the expected UNRRA $2 billion budget. The total U.S. contribution to UNRRA operations amounted to 73 per cent of the funds available between March 28, 1944 and July 23, 1946. (George Woodbridge, *UNRRA: History of UN Relief and Rehabilitation Administration*. New York: Columbia University, 1950, Vol. I, pp. 1-13.) Most of the specific projects to which the U.S. objected involved the Soviet Union in one way or another. The USSR received large assistance from UNRRA, while some countries—notably Austria, Korea, and Formosa—received no assistance, and others—notably Italy—were receiving insufficient amounts. The U.S. also objected to UNRRA's support to refugee operations, especially those involving peoples being involuntarily repatriated in East European countries.

There are strict limits to the amount of authority that one government can exercise over the activities of others, even those financed by foreign aid.

Where aid has to take the form of grants, therefore, Congress prefers the outright commodity gift because it is not easily transferable among different economic sectors. Agricultural surpluses used for relief purposes, for example, are very likely to reach their intended destination, provided the foods involved are appropriate and acceptable. Only rarely have relief foods been used indirectly to encourage or permit activities not contemplated in the original grant. It is true, however, that the shipment of grains or other raw materials may relieve the beneficiary government from having to spend its scarce foreign exchange for these needed commodities; and also that this gives it the option of spending its unused foreign currencies on consumer luxuries or on capital equipment. Thus, even United States surplus wheat may make it theoretically possible for importers in Saigon or Vientiane to buy perfume or Cadillacs, or for the government involved to support questionable projects.[7] And there have been shipments of American wheat that have enabled the beneficiary to export its own food—sometimes, as in 1965 in the UAR, to Communist customers.[8]

In this sense, any form of capital aid may conceivably contribute to uses of which the United States disapproves. Even military hardware offered under a defense agreement may release national resources for other purposes in the receiving country. This "fungibility" or interchangeability of resources within underdeveloped countries creates one of the strongest political complaints against any form of capital assistance.

Grants versus Loans

Offering aid in the form of project loans is one popular solution to the problems of control and fungibility. Loans have to be repaid; therefore, they are expected to support only activities of economic value. Because they are made for specific projects, they create an impression of credit worthiness and solidity rather than political expediency; and loans do not seem to imply American support to either the projects or the regimes involved, since they can be treated as a business proposition. Loans are therefore easier than grants to justify to Congress. They also seem more economical because they do not have to be written off at the outset as a dead loss. Even before the establishment of the De-

---

[7] The economic significance of substituting agricultural commodities for dollar aid is explored in Lawrence Witt and Carl Eicher, *The Effects of U.S. Agricultural Surplus Disposal Programs on Recipient Countries* (East Lansing, Mich.: State University Dept. of Agricultural Economics, 1964).

[8] *The New York Times,* June 15, 1965.

velopment Loan Fund in the Mutual Security Act of 1957, there were indications that Congress was ready to abandon grants-in-aid; and with each passing year thereafter, aid agencies were urged to persuade other nations to apply for development loans rather than grants, and to help prepare applications for various forms of credit.

The notion that loans are more businesslike than grants should not be carried too far. It overlooks the reasons why capital aid exists at all. Projects with an obvious economic justification are not ordinarily eligible for foreign aid; indeed, under prevailing legislation and administrative practice, loans that can be commercially financed are referred to banks and other development funds. "Soft" loans (those made on easy-payment terms) must still be made on the basis of a country's balance-of-payments position; and some are so "soft" that they have been estimated to be 80 per cent gifts. Moreover, it has still been necessary to offer general or program (rather than specific project) support to some countries. For such reasons, regardless of the credit worthiness of individual projects for which money is lent, the developing countries may never be able to repay their foreign loans in full. The Latin American countries in the Alliance for Progress found by the end of 1964 that they had external debts of over $10 billion, nearly half of which was due for repayment within five years. India's foreign debt service was 17 per cent of the nation's total foreign exchange earnings, a figure that might double within the coming decade if India continues to borrow the capital necessary for planned development. Repayment of debts on foreign loans was already becoming a major factor in development financing in 1955, when 8 per cent of the external assistance received by these countries was offset by debt service. But by 1964, after ten years of increasing emphasis on loans, debt service offset 30 per cent of all foreign aid, rising from $800 million yearly in 1956 to $3.5 billion in 1964. No doubt further loans can be made to permit debt servicing, but it is not certain how far the rate of economic development will permit the liquidation of such obligations without undue strain on the national resources. In the last analysis, aid for economic purposes ought to be offered on the basis of need and capacity, not ability to repay; indeed, sometimes the two are inversely related:[9] The less a country is able to repay, the more it may stand in need of aid.

The War Loans Experience

Some of the problems of relying on public loans as the major instrument for capital transfers can be illuminated by citing the discouraging American experiences with wartime loans. United States loans to

[9] See John P. Lewis, *The Quiet Crises in India* (New York: Doubleday, Anchor Books, 1964), Chap. XII; Edward S. Mason, *Foreign Aid and Foreign Policy* (New York: Harper & Row, 1964), Chap. I and pp. 61-70.

France during World War I, for example, resulted in sharp exchanges of diplomatic and popular asperity between the two countries. Yet originally it had been the United States Congress that had planned to make an outright grant to France, nominally in recognition of its aid to the United States during the Revolutionary War,[10] and it was the French Premier who had requested loans instead of grants, to avoid injuring the national pride. The argument from national pride closely parallels contemporary discussions of the superiority of loans over grants. But loans to a government in need of capital may only defer the injury to be suffered by national pride. In this case, not many years passed before the United States Treasury was voicing unpleasant sentiments about the repayment of the Liberty Loans, and the French Government was protesting its inability to oblige.[11] In 1924, the French

[10] French assistance to the U.S. during the Revolutionary War included some $6.3 million in loans between 1778 and 1783. These were repaid in 1795; yet secret French aid to the Colonies, the "lost millions" of Beaumarchais, and similar issues kept recurring for more than a generation in Franco-American negotiations and congressional debates. French aid also included grants: the troops sent by France in support of the American Revolution received their supplies from French sources, and Benjamin Franklin's offer to provide logistical support to them was politely refused. Moreover, even though most of the French assistance took the form of loans, they were discharged at an interest of 5 per cent, although the French government itself paid 7 per cent for the capital. Additionally, outright gifts amounting to something under $2 million were also given. (See *Our Debt to France*. New York: Washington-Lafayette Institute, Inc., 1926, pp. 8-13, 44. See also Feis, *Diplomacy of the Dollar*, p. 22; Brown and Opie, *American Foreign Assistance*, p. 2.)

Great Britain retaliated for French support to the American Revolution by financing its European allies against France during the Napoleonic Wars. In this case, most of the support was through direct subsidies. There were some exceptions: an important loan of £4.6 million to the Emperor of Germany (1794-1796), which was guaranteed; £1.62 million to the Emperor was not repaid, however, and much of it was used to pay interest on the first loan. A £600,000 loan to Portugal, made in 1809, was only partially repaid. A £200,000 loan to the Dutch royal house in 1813 was repaid, as was a £2,000 loan to the French Bourbons in 1814. On the other hand, subsidies were given to Austria, Russia, Prussia, Bavaria, Hanover, Hesse-Cassel, and other German states, Sweden, Sicily, Sardinia, Portugal, and French Émigrés Corps. For more details, see Norman J. Silberling, "Financial and Monetary Policy of Great Britain during the Napoleonic Wars," *Quarterly Journal of Economics*, XXXVIII, No. 2 (Feb., 1924), 214-33.

In World War I, Britain borrowed $4 billion from the U.S. but lent $8 billion to its allies. Afterward, the British offered to cancel their loans if the U.S. would do likewise—a paper loss of $4 billion. The U.S. insisted on full payment, and the British struggled with their debts, trying to collect from debtors and depending on German reparations which, in turn, were financed by private U.S. loans to Germany. (Bruce Russett, *Community and Contention*. Cambridge, Mass.: M.I.T., 1963, p. 12.)

[11] The French budgetary analysis in *Inventaire de la situation financière de la France au début de la troisième législature presenté par M. Clemente Ministre des Finances*, Paris, 1924. (Feis, *Diplomacy of the Dollar*.) The issue is not dead, except financially: Senator William Fulbright, objecting to President de Gaulle's insistence on an independent foreign policy for France, cited the unpaid World War I loans of $4.3 billion as evidence of American long-term commitment to European integrity. (*The New York Times*, Oct. 30, 1963.)

budget had contained no reference at all to the war debts to Britain or the United States; national pride still had to be set aside, and the loans were now regarded as "general pooling of war expenditures" among the allies.[12]

As American isolationists never failed to remark during the early internationalism of the New Deal, most European World War I debts were never repaid in full. But the political and perhaps economic impossibility of paying off the war debts and reparations did not discourage Americans from undertaking aid to its Allies in World War II along similar lines of credit and exchange. The original concept of lend-lease was a reaffirmation of the United States preference for making loans instead of grants to friendly countries in need of aid.

It is tempting to equate intergovernmental loans with private debts; but the analogy is a false one. In terms of national economic prosperity, the consequences of repaying loans made in either World War would have been harmful to the creditors as well as to the debtors.[13] And if the industrialized western allies have been unable to repay dollar loans made during a period of crisis, the capacity of the underdeveloped countries to do so—especially if the loans are large enough to make the desired economic impact—is all the more questionable.

Foreign Aid Loans

In spite of the historical reasons for doubting the fiscal soundness of international loans, the United States Congress has favored the banking approach to aid. The reasons for this preference are partly ideological and partly pragmatic.

Aid loans are extended with a minimum of burden on the borrowers, including provisions for a period of grace that permits the

[12] Louis Marin took the floor of the Chamber of Deputies to explain in resentful language the French position on repayment: "While war still raged, statesmen in every country appealed to the common cause. Some gave their ships, some munitions, some the lives of their sons, some money, and today only those who gave money come saying to us: 'Give back what we loaned.'"

[13] After surveying the flow of debt obligations and international trade between the wars, a famous Brookings Institution study concluded that the payment of debts from the poor to the rich would retard European development and thus injure the U.S.: "A complete obliteration of all reparation and war debt obligations would promote, rather than retard, world economic prosperity. . . . Even if collection could be made, the results would be harmful. The collection of these inter-governmental debts would be economically detrimental, rather than beneficial, to the creditor country." (Harold G. Moulton and Leo Pasvolsky, *War Debts and World Prosperity*. Washington: Brookings, 1932, p. 422.) Indeed, the best progress "toward financial and economic stability" in Europe occurred from 1924-1929, when under the Dawes plan there was a "net flow of wealth from the United States to the impoverished nations of Europe and particularly to Germany." (*Ibid.*, pp. 421, 420.)

debtors to wait as long as ten years before beginning to pay off the principal. Even the interest rates (ranging down to ¾ of 1 per cent in some years) have sometimes been too low to cover the service costs or the prospect of inflation over the very long period (as long as 40 years) for which some loans are extended.

Congressional preference for loans rests partly on their psychological advantage over outright grants. Even a mythical obligation to repay is a caution against waste. Loan projects must be carefully designed, and presumably they are reviewed on technical and economic grounds rather than poltical considerations.[14] Yet it is sometimes difficult for the borrowing government to accept the strictness of American supervision over loan projects: many American technicians have reported difficulty in answering the question, "Why do you care how efficiently we carry out this project? It's really our money, once we have agreed to repay it." But there is no doubt that in many situations, both the United States government and the host country have been more careful in administering "borrowed" dollars than gifts.

The ideological reasons for the congressional preference remain, however. There is still a general distrust of handouts, and a hope that loans will be less of a burden on the United States taxpayer than outright grants. There is also the political advantage that loans seem more businesslike than grants.[15]

Direct capital flows remain the major component of foreign aid, however difficult it has become to distinguish between loans and grants, or between commercial and other components. Recent developments have not reduced the importance of capital aid, but only added to the resources available to increase its effectiveness.

HUMAN RESOURCE DEVELOPMENT

Capital aid may serve only part—and sometimes not the most urgent part—of the developing countries' pressing needs. It is suitable where the basic human resources for using it already exist, including the engineers and economists to develop projects, the managers to administer them, the technicians to operate them, and skilled workers to build, maintain, and manage them. Capital development depends upon human development.

Although it is obvious that dollars alone cannot induce economic

[14] This is also a somewhat mythical distinction, since loans are usually related to American interests in the country involved. In 1962, it would doubtless have been harder for Guinea or Ghana than for Nigeria to get American aid loans, even if the projects themselves were identical.

[15] The economic weakness of the argument for loans is explored in Robert E. Asher, *Grants, Loans, and Local Currencies* (Washington: Brookings, 1961).

development, the implications of this fact are easily overlooked. The concept of treating uneducated and unskilled humanity as a national resource capable of systematic development is novel and in some ways uncomfortable. Among other things, it implies an effort to educate and motivate man on a larger scale than ever before in history.

Perhaps technical assistance as a foreign operation began with the discovery by Christian missionaries that (martyrdom aside) piety prospers better in societies that have begun to reduce physical misery, and it was not long before the mission of preaching began to include an important element of teaching. In the larger sense, technical assistance is as old as humanity, for it is now well established that even the most casual cultural contacts among peoples frequently result in some technological interchange. Important discoveries have been traced from society to society as far back as man has lived in organized groups. Technical assistance may be classed as an advanced form of acculturation, distinguished by the fact that it represents a deliberate and planned attempt to improve the technology of another people.[16]

Apart from the brief colonial experience in the Philippines, the United States has had little interest or experience in cultural aggrandizement. During World War II, however, the Reconstruction Finance Corporation began to offer large-scale technical assistance and specialized training to speed up the production of strategic raw materials in Latin America; and by the end of 1941, the Coordinator of Inter-American Affairs was offering technical assistance as well as other cultural and information activities in public health, education, and agriculture. But these operations never assumed very substantial proportions, and even the United Nations Relief and Rehabilitation Administration in postwar Europe did not include much technical assistance. What these forerunners of modern foreign aid contributed to the era of the Marshall Plan was a pool of experience from which to draw.[17]

The Marshall Plan era did not reveal the need for technical assistance that was to develop during the 1950's. Yet even European recovery was already providing evidence that capital assistance would not be enough. The destruction of Europe's capital plant had made it

---

[16] See George M. Foster, *Traditional Cultures and the Impact of Technological Change* (New York: Harper & Row, 1960).

[17] During the wartime period, technical assistance to Latin America cost only $5 million. In the three years that followed World War II, another $7 million was spent on technical assistance in the area. (Brown and Opie, *American Foreign Assistance*, pp. 82, 116.) UNRRA operations included technical assistance in agriculture and industry to modernize facilities and increase productivity to a level adequate to support the population. (See Woodbridge, *UNRRA: The History of U.N. Relief*, II, 17, 18, 31, 32.) The most extensive programs were in veterinary techniques, transportation, construction, and equipment maintenance, antimalarial and other public health campaigns, and training in the use of machinery.

necessary to replace worn-out and obsolete equipment with the latest manufacturing innovations, but it soon appeared that upgrading the old technicians and changing a war production program to a consumer-minded economy required more than money. A variety of technical assistance programs was soon underway, usually on a small, information-supplying basis. The Marshall Plan's European productivity centers, for example, provided exchanges of advice, and the Question-and-Answer Service under the Department of Commerce in the early 1950's referred specific technical assistance questions to American experts for written answers. The Economic Cooperation Administration also organized a technical division that had $21 million allotted to it by fiscal year 1950. What was happening in Europe was simply a large-scale application of the management and industrial consulting techniques that had developed in the United States.

The deceptively easy success of the Marshall Plan did not fully prepare the industrialized nations for the challenges that lay ahead. By the end of 1951, the European Recovery Program had generally achieved its purposes six months ahead of its own deadline, at a cost of only $12 billion instead of the $17 billion anticipated.[18] But the Korean War was a reminder that industrial rehabilitation for peacetime prosperity was not enough to prevent the Cold War from becoming hot in other parts of the world. The United States found that it would have to increase its influence in the underdeveloped areas where the USSR was to begin an increasingly successful propaganda offensive.

Establishing significant relations with the underdeveloped countries required new forms of aid diplomacy, more intimate association with national planning and resource allocation in other countries, and greater involvement in the effort to develop human technological and managerial capacities. Aid began to require the presence of large staffs of technicians, first to help develop suitable projects, and then to help carry them out.

Technical assistance was now viewed as a "multiplier" activity, and each technician was expected to be more a teacher than a doer. The impossibility of using foreign capital alone to move the developing countries immediately to an industrial age was hinted by the first rough estimate of the cost: $19 billion a year to increase their national income a mere 2 per cent annually.[19] Such sums could hardly be even contemplated from American or other Western sources; and if they could have been provided, they could not have been usefully absorbed in the underdeveloped societies that so desperately wanted them. Many ex-

[18] Brown and Opie, *American Foreign Assistance*, p. 569.
[19] U.N., *Measures for Economic Development of Underdeveloped Countries*, May, 1951, p. 76.

colonial nations were suspicious of foreign investment and distrustful of capitalism in any form. The initiative was therefore left to each government, which, in turn, had few technicians and still fewer innovators available to implement its aspirations. But since the government of the developing country held the keys to power, it alone could open the door. President Truman's "bold new program" was the first to stand at the threshhold.

The Presidential inaugural address of 1949 marked the official introduction of the coordinated large-scale program of technical assistance. Point Four in President Truman's program declared:

> . . . we must embark on a bold new program for making the benefits of our scientific advances and industrial progress available for the improvement and growth of underdeveloped areas. . . . For the first time in history, humanity possesses the knowledge and skill to relieve the sufferings of these people . . . our imponderable resources in technical knowledge are constantly growing and are inexhaustible.

The optimism of these early Point Four days grew from the concept that unlike capital, knowledge may be shared without being diminished.

Sharing this "inexhaustible" fund of American knowledge required changing the administrative approach to foreign aid. Capital loans and grants required only small teams, sometimes working on a transient basis, to administer them. But offering technical assistance to countries that lacked an adequately educated base meant that groups of technicians had to be introduced into each country, covering many fields, in cooperation with counterpart officials from the host government. Aid missions began to grow in size, and Americans began to work closely with technicians at all levels of government in the developing countries. The cost of this program was still small—only $35 million was authorized in the first act (1950)—but technical innovations and anticipated improvements in the climate for private investment were expected to attract private capital for additional development purposes. Technical assistance was offered in the early years in irrigation and water control, food and agriculture, rural improvement, malaria control, public health, sanitation, education, natural resources, housing, transportation, commerce, industry, marketing, and public administration. By 1963, the Agency for International Development, still following the lines of the "bold new program," was stationing 3,000 of its own technicians abroad, engaged primarily in training and demonstration. Under government contracts, 70 American colleges and universities had teams overseas in education, agriculture, public administration, public health, and industrial development; cooperatives and labor unions were also engaged in housing, credit, marketing, and other fields. Technicians under private contract and on loan from other government agencies brought the total to 5,000.[20] Yet only 8 per cent of AID funds (15 per cent of its economic development budget) was assigned to technical assistance; and even in 1965, the United States was probably supplying fewer than 15 per cent of the 100,000 technical assistants at work in the underdeveloped world.

The United States was fairly launched in the use of technical assistance to supplement the capital requirements of development and respond to the immediately pressing human resource problems of economic development. But technical assistance posed problems entirely different from those involved in the capital assistance of the preceding era.

Problems of Technical Assistance

American technicians assigned to advise governments in the developing countries soon found that they were playing dual and conflicting roles. In releasing funds to projects on which they were advising, they found themselves exercising an authority far greater than that of a counselor. Under such conditions, advice often became a command. A technician who felt that his suggestions were being ignored or overruled was tempted to urge that funds be cut off because the project was being inefficiently administered. Moreover, United States personnel were usually rotated to other posts every two years, especially in the early years of Point Four, and changes in technicians often meant changes in technique. Administrators and officials of the host government as well were—and sometimes still are—rotated rapidly among jobs, especially if they proved capable enough to merit promotion.

Technical assistance also meant the sharing of techniques on a person-to-person basis, a process that was not fast enough to satisfy the needs of the developing countries. Sometimes the shortage of technicians in the host government meant that the American expert had to work alone, or with an untrained counterpart; in other cases a single overworked official had to become the "counterpart" of two or three Americans, each of whom was trying to proffer advice on his own project without reference to its implications for other sectors of the developing society. The strain of attempting to reconcile this sometimes conflicting advice, while at the same time participating in a novel development program, often forced the harassed administrators in the developing countries to make decisions haphazardly and arbitrarily. In whatever sectors foreign aid was being offered, large-scale increases in

[20] AID, *The Role of Technical Assistance in Foreign Aid,* April, 1963, pp. 4-6; AID, *Operations Report,* March 31, 1964, p. 48; and *Foreign Aid Program, Annual Report to Congress for FY 1963,* p. 8. By June 30, 1965, no fewer than 125 colleges and universities had $195 million in 293 separate contracts for technical services.

technical manpower seemed to be necessary in order to enable the host government to act at all.

The Manpower Approach to Educational Development

It became obvious almost at once that technical assistance had to be accompanied by manpower development on a large scale. For these reasons, technical assistants working in United States aid missions began to seek out ways of relating their expertise to the educational system as a whole. The improvement of the national educational system to accommodate the requirements of a modernizing society was not merely a matter of injecting the appropriate technologies into the secondary and collegiate curriculum. It was necessary to provide teachers in technical schools and teacher-training colleges, to supply capital grants for libraries and laboratories, and to establish vocational education and agricultural schools. And even these efforts did not satisfy the insistent demand for mass education in traditional subjects.

The educational requirements in Africa alone were of staggering proportions. In May 1961, when ministers of education met in Addis Ababa to coordinate their efforts throughout the continent, they found that it was going to cost up to $1 billion a year by 1970 to provide universal primary education, secondary education for 30 per cent of the primary graduates, and higher education for 20 per cent of the high school graduates. An additional 163,000 teachers would be needed for primary education alone during the period of 1965-1970; and even then the immediate need for trained manpower would still be unfilled. For secondary education in 1961-1966, some 63,000 new teachers would have to be found. When it is recalled that these figures still did not take into account the fact that most of the present teachers in Africa were insufficiently qualified, supplying only Africa's manpower development needs in the near future appeared all but impossible.[21] It became evident that a drastic breakthrough in the technology of mass education, or drastic revisions in the expectations of the developing countries, would be necessary.

Participant Training

Human resource development required the introduction of other means for providing an adequate supply of trained manpower. The

[21] A study at the Netherlands Economic Institute concluded that 6,000 university teachers would have to be sent to the underdeveloped countries before 1970 and that 8,000 to 10,000 "teachers of teachers" would be needed before 1965 to work in teacher-training colleges. (See Ladislav Cerych, *Problems of Aid to Education in Developing Countries* (New York: Praeger, 1965).

most important of these was the opening of American and European universities to students from Latin America, the Middle East, Africa, and Asia. Some 50,000 students were enrolled in Western Europe and North America in 1958-1959, in addition to 7,000 in the Soviet Union and 3,500 in Japan.[22] The United States took in the largest proportion of students—38 per cent, as opposed to 14 per cent in France, 12 per cent in Germany, and 9 per cent in the United Kingdom. The American education system was able to absorb still more students, however: the proportion of foreign students to total college and university enrollments (only 1.45 per cent) was lower in the United States than in the United Kingdom (10.7 per cent), France (7.7 per cent), or Germany (9.2 per cent), because the United States has a much larger proportion of its own college-age population enrolled in higher education.

In addition to formal enrollments of students from developing countries in American colleges and universities, large numbers were brought to the United States under special Participant Training programs. A total of 70,556 trainees were sponsored under AID and predecessor programs from 1950-1963, and another 180,000 foreign nationals had been trained in the United States by July, 1964, under military assistance programs.[23] The participant training programs of both AID and the Military Assistance Program were usually organized in connection with specific development or military projects.[24]

Designing programs to serve human resource development needs requires analysis similar to that used in determining a country's capital needs. The 1961 Act for International Development provided, in fact,

[22] The estimates refer to members of the Organization for European Corporation and Development (OECD): Austria, Belgium, Canada, Denmark, France, the Federal Republic of Germany, Greece, Iceland, Ireland, Italy, Luxembourg, Netherlands, Norway, Portugal, Spain, Sweden, Switzerland, Turkey, the United Kingdom, and the United States. These figures appear in OECD, *Policy Conference on Economic Growth and Investment in Education, V: The Flows of Students,* February, 1962, p. 11.

[23] The average training period of the AID programs was 9 months. (AID, International Training Division, *Training and Development,* 3rd ed., 1963), pp. 3-6.) Of these, 27.4 per cent were in industry, mining, and transportation, and 13.7 per cent in agriculture. Over the whole period, 24.3 per cent came from Latin America, and 23.5 per cent from the Far East. By fiscal year 1963, however, 40 per cent were coming from Latin America, and 20 per cent from Africa. All these figures exclude those sent under university contracts with the Agency for International Development. The figures for military assistance programs appear in *Hearings Before the Senate Committee on Foreign Relations, Foreign Assistance Act of 1963,* 88th Cong., 1st sess., 1963, p. 177. In addition to the military nations trained as participants, another 54,000 were to have been trained over the same period at American installations abroad.

[24] AID, International Training Division, *Participant Training Program—How It Works,* June, 1962, pp. 1, 6. Much of this participant training also takes place at colleges and universities, but the largest proportion is with suitable government agencies at all levels.

that capital aid should not receive a high priority "until the requisite knowledge and skills had been developed." The American programs of recent years have increasingly used the human resource approach in determining priorities. Thus in 40 countries, development grants (largely in education) and technical assistance for human resource development have accounted for more than 50 per cent of the total United States assistance. In countries where human resources necessary for technical and economic progress have already been well developed, such as in India and in Pakistan, these forms of aid amounted to less than 5 per cent of the United States total; in Japan, Israel, Spain and Greece, United States technical assistance has been discontinued as no longer necessary. In still other situations, where the countries' need for trained manpower was so great that their scarce technicians could not be spared even for further training or for collaboration with American counterparts, the United States began to supply operating personnel through the Peace Corps and voluntary agencies.

The range of resources applied to the human element in development by American aid agencies thus offered even more flexibility than that of the capital component of foreign aid.

United Nations Programs

United Nations efforts in human resource development, although smaller than those of the United States, have provided an important and highly flexible instrument of technical assistance. The 1945 United Nations charter meeting in San Francisco had created the Economic and Social Council and pledged all member nations to promote higher living standards and economic development (Articles 55 and 56). But the technical assistance did not become an important United Nations operation until President Truman had given his Point Four address. A few months after the Truman address, the Secretary General proposed an Expanded Program of Technical Assistance, which reached $4.5 million in 1950 and $54.7 in 1964. The United Nations program offered aid to 130 countries or territories in 1964. Fellowships, scholarships, seminars, conferences, pilot and demonstration projects, technical writing and equipment were made available, and technical experts were sent individually and in groups upon request of the member governments. The principal advantage of the United Nations' approach was that it had access to technicians from all member states, and on several occasions underdeveloped countries themselves were able to supply technicians for the benefit of another member. This enabled them to retain a sense of dignity in requesting technical advice, since their role was also that of a donor. Within a few years, most of the member states had contributed staff members and technicians to the United Nations Technical Assistance Administration.[25]

United Nations technicians in the field have experienced problems similar to those encountered by Americans. An international organization has important advantages over the bilateral programs of the United States, however, since the provision of services to members preserves an appearance of mutuality that is difficult to sustain in bilateral operations. On the other hand, there are also administrative disadvantages in the United Nations' style of operation: technicians recruited from various parts of the world work with different national approaches that are sometimes difficult to harmonize within a project; individuals working on a series of temporary assignments do not enjoy the same degree of career security that can be offered in an American Foreign Service post; and finally, United Nations technicians serve as individuals thinly scattered among 1,500 separate projects, rather than as members of a large team working on an integrated program. In the field, the UN agency that supplies the technicians prescribes their approach. They work without the support of integrated country planning and logistical services unless these are supplied by the host nation. On the other hand, UN operations are sometimes more flexible and imaginative than those in a large, coordinated, bilateral aid mission. Even before the U.S. Peace Corps was established, the UN began to supply "operatives" to supplement the work of advisers, especially in Africa. Under this program, senior administrators and technicians became available to replace departing colonial administrators and specialists. Operational, executive, and administrative (OPEX) personnel were supplied by the UN Office of Public Administration, to be temporarily "integrated" into the service of the beneficiary government.[26]

Whether performed by bilateral agencies or by the United Nations, programs in human resource development may bring about an uncomfortably close involvement in important aspects of domestic politics. Even the use of foreign officials and expatriates—which is recognized as a temporary, emergency solution, providing local skilled

[25] See especially H. L. Keenleyside, "Administrative Problems of the U.N. Technical Assistance Administration," *Public Administration*, XXXIII, Autumn, 1955, pp. 241-67.

[26] Walter R. Sharp, *Field Administration in the United Nations System* (New York: Praeger, 1961), pp. 194N, 399. Professor Sharp's book includes useful descriptions of technical assistance operations in general, as well as of UN procedures. See especially pp. 295-448. The evaluation on pp. 449-501 is an introduction to the potentialities and weaknesses of technical assistance. A good discussion of problems of technical assistance operations in the field will also be found in Morris E. Opler, *Social Aspects of Technical Assistance in Operation* (Paris: UNESCO, 1954), pp. 42-51. See also John D. Montgomery, "Crossing the Culture Bars," *World Politics*, XII, No. 4 (July, 1961).

manpower necessary for modernizing a society in transition—exposes them to sensitive governmental operations. Temporary manpower from external sources and local training in skills for long-term application sitll do not equip a society for its twentieth century needs.

SOCIAL RESOURCE DEVELOPMENT

As early as 1958, Harlan Cleveland applied the term "institution-building" to the effort to develop an organizational context for technical skills and knowledge necessary to modernization. In the mid-1950's there had been a rash of stories about foreign aid bulldozers rusting away near areas that were being cleared with coolie labor—rusting because there were no drivers, mechanics, or spare parts to keep machinery moving; and about foreign aid pumps lying unused because the villagers, seeing no advantage in abandoning their traditional use of river water, made no provisions to maintain or operate them. Similar instances were found in technical assistance operations throughout the world. Many failures were ascribed to techniques that were incompatible with traditions of other peoples: American agriculturalists had made effective use of extension services to increase individual farmers' productivity in the United States, for example, but these same techniques did not always succeed abroad, because they clashed with other governments' attitudes toward their citizens, or with attitudes of farmers toward foreign technicians and foreign ways. Many ambitious projects that appeared well launched and self-justifying collapsed as soon as the American technicians left and their counterparts were promoted or transferred to other tasks.

It is now clear that modernization is a social process. Neither capital increments nor technical changes alone account for the difference between underdeveloped and modern industrial societies. To have a continuing impact, foreign aid has to concern itself deeply with the social, political, cultural, and total economic context in which it operates overseas.

The concepts of institution-building and social development have not yet been clearly defined, and even the terms are still controversial. In various forms, such operations have always been associated with foreign aid, which has had the effect of strengthening, weakening, or building institutions that receive capital and technical assistance. When a technician trains a counterpart to carry on his work after he leaves, he is trying to 'institutionalize" knowledge. When a new office or bureau is created to perform the same functions, knowledge has greater life expectancy. If a law is passed requiring citizens to act in certain unaccustomed ways, the institutions of a society may be forced to adjust still more permanently to accommodate changed situations. Some institutions—schools, industries, and commercial enterprises—have a physical existence and are to some degree self-perpetuating. But institutions that are to introduce and sustain economic development must modernize the habits of masses of people. Creating or changing institutions for purposes of modernization requires a large measure of involvement in the internal affairs of the developing nation.[27]

Several approaches to institutional change have emerged from American overseas operations. After World War II, efforts were made to introduce institutions that would destroy fascism and encourage democracy in the occupied nations. Aid and advice were offered to government agencies at all levels; laws were passed in Japan, altering even the family relationships and protecting a new status for women; governmental services, the educational system, and the industrial and commercial economy were reorganized and private land was transferred to individual peasant farmers. The success of these technical innovations depended upon the eventual fate of the institutions established during the military occupation. Once military force was withdrawn, only the acceptance of the new order by the people and their leaders would protect the innovations.

Even under the Marshall Plan, which was primarily a capital assistance program, there were important efforts at institution-building. One such device was the merging of European and American funds in projects of mutual interest, which gave American advisers a chance to participate in discussions of economic development plans while they left the final responsibilities to the Europeans themselves. This collaboration among American and European planners made possible the development of international planning and finally contributed to such institutions at the European Payments Union, the European Coal and Steel Community, the Organization for Economic Cooperation and Development, and the Common Market. Thus the injection of capital became an instrument of collaboration and the means of building institutions capable of tremendous adaptation and creativity.

Applying the institution-building approach to underdeveloped countries is a still more formidable task. In Europe and Japan, institutions had been built in modern, industrialized societies possessing not only an abundance of technical and managerial talent, but also attitudes and habits consistent with economic rationality and with political and administrative efficiency. In the developing world, basic social changes had to occur where none of these conditions prevailed. Moreover, the

[27] The *servicios* in Latin America and the Sino-American Joint Commission for Rural Reconstruction, dating from the 1940's, were successful in building institutions for the transfer of technical knowledge. U.S. support to them was terminated in the 1960's (see Chap. 4).

leverage available to the modernizing forces was much less than that of the military government or of the Marshall Plan statesmen with their resources of large-scale capital aid (most of the capital aid to under-developed countries was small in amount, except where it was related to military requirements). Technical assistants had to work through counterpart technicians in the host government. A few saw the advantages of introducing administrative and legal supports to their work, of popularizing new approaches, and of encouraging governmental and public attitudes favorable to social and economic development. Good technical assistants adopted institution-building approaches almost by instinct, but their opportunities for so doing were few and isolated.

Apart from exceptional cases in which institution-building resulted from individual initiative, most technical assistants generally assumed that modernization was a matter of technology. For them there was a minimum of involvement in the internal concerns of the host government, even when they were directly related to development. Technicians came and went on their two-year terms, which were sometimes renewed but often were not; projects were often designed, or at least subject to revision in each detail, by experts in Washington, thousands of miles from the scene; and shifting personnel, new laws, administrative and organizational changes, and domestic pressures from the United States and the host government diverted aid projects in a variety of directions without regard to their impact on local institutions. Visitors to American technical assistance operations overseas were constantly impressed with signs of impermanence, with the evidence of technicians and techniques transferred from place to place without regard to local differences, and with frustrations that developed over projects suddenly infused with political implications. Newly arrived technicians always seemed enthusiastic about their prospects, ignoring or denigrating what had gone before, but confident (on the surface, at least) that the solution had just been found and that progress was about to begin. This peculiar feeling of excitement that accompanied technical assistance operations during the 1950's struck many observers as disproportionate to the achievements already on record. Students of foreign aid began to suspect that the failure lay in considering questions of technique and money as the only highways to the twentieth century, without regard for the institutions that had to be transformed or the populations whose attitudes and skills had to be drastically changed.

One reason for the despair of the late 1950's over the prospects of foreign aid was the difficulty of institution-building in unfavorable situations. As Chapter 3 will suggest, some students of foreign aid argued that no United States financial or technical assistance at all should be given to countries lacking the will or capacity to establish social conditions leading to progress. Governments of stagnant countries would only misuse aid, according to this theory; and it was even suggested that aid would produce conditions of instability and unrest if it were used for the benefit of unproductive or socially reactionary minorities.

One of the first tasks of foreign aid strategists, therefore, remains to examine the nature of development and to decide in what circumstances United States aid can reasonably be expected to contribute to general economic growth and to the social and political order that United States foreign policy is attempting to promote.

3

Tactics of Foreign Aid

A noted writer on international affairs argued against offering foreign aid to certain countries because, according to him, just as "there are bums and beggars, so there are bum and beggar nations." [1] The implication of this argument is that there is a fixed ordering of nations, and of men, some with special virtues that are denied to others; and that whether these gifts take the form of an inheritance or of energy and ability in people, they have their counterparts in national affairs: natural resources or national will and leadership. This view sees little that can be done to change one's (or a nation's) condition.

Nowhere in the argument is there any attempt to identify the nations that are the bums and beggars. If dependence on external assistance is a basis for this classification, developing countries like Israel, Taiwan, and Greece would have to be included. They received aid even though their gross national product increased 10 per cent, 7.5 per cent, and 6 per cent, respectively, over the past decade. India would be a beggar because it remained poor even though 83 per cent of its gross investment was provided out of its own resources, yet it still required heavy aid from the United States. And doubtless Vietnam would have been abandoned as a bum years ago because its beginnings at economic restoration, after nearly two decades of war, had become a signal for a vigorous guerrilla offensive. Once this formula is applied to nations

[1] Hans J. Morgenthau, "Preface to a Political Theory of Foreign Aid," in *Why Foreign Aid?* ed. Robert A. Goldwyn (Chicago: Rand McNally, 1962), p. 79.

like these, the need for a more searching inquiry is obvious: the real task is to identify the causes of growth and stagnation, if possible, and then relate them to the capabilities of foreign aid, rather than to apply an Oriental fatalism to nations that have difficulty coping with the demands of modernization.

Both psychology and history challenge the implication that some nations—even the most apparently static—are doomed to remain changeless. Individuals have moved from rags to riches in both fiction and life, and back again. Nations ruled by corrupt governments have been reborn, while great and well-managed empires and democracies have decayed to the state of national beggary. No great power can afford to assume that the present order of world politics is permanent.

Whether external aid can contribute to the improvement of a nation's condition is a factual question. It is obvious that democracy cannot be purchased and installed like missile bases, but certain specific economic and technical improvements can be introduced almost anywhere. Secretary of State George C. Marshall's plan for "the revival of a working economy in the world" was designed to "permit the emergence of political and social conditions in which free institutions can exist." This ambitious program was not intended to be universal. The plan succeeded in Europe, where American aid restored greatness to nations already possessing the essential skills and determination. And experiences in the underdeveloped nations have demonstrated that capital, technology, and even the capability for planning and administering development can be supplied as well (given the motivation to change). It is only when such motivation and leadership are lacking that one is tempted to think of some nations as bums and beggars. The temptation is a dangerous one, for if bums and beggars are too long neglected, their destructive potential may be enormous. Foreign aid, from a variety of sources, is therefore concentrated at some points and remains on a token scale at others. The expectations in some cases will be significant economic improvement, in others an increased capacity to protect the state against destruction, and in still others no more than a temporary stay affording working time and postponing crucial decisions to a more hopeful future.

Foreign aid assumes that the injection of resources external to a developing society may be used to *stabilize, speed,* or *influence* change. On many occasions, in fact, aid programs attempt to serve all three objectives at once in various sectors of the developing society. Since each of these purposes calls for different tactics, the problem of reconciling them in a single country is a complex one.

The tactics used to stabilize a society undergoing change involve supporting the forces of order, such as the army, the police, bureaucratic governmental institutions, and sometimes political elements of a strong conservative persuasion. These tactics are used in a wide variety of situations in which short-term stability seems necessary in order to permit long-run change to occur peaceably. The most urgent of these situations are those presenting a serious threat of external invasion or internal insurgency where Communist forces are awaiting the opportunity to strike—for example, in Thailand. Stabilizing tactics are also used, with less success, where American investments need protection (notably in the extractive industries, and especially those having military or strategic importance)—as in Iran. Finally, in the least promising of situations, they are used where American aid of marginal size is considered necessary in order to preserve communications with a regime in power that is otherwise considered undeserving of aid—as in Haiti.

The tactics used to speed economic development have received the most serious attention from the American public and scholarly community: indeed, they are often described as the only appropriate use of foreign aid. At present, programs designed for economic development absorb the largest element of foreign aid, including many large-scale projects in transportation, irrigation, and power, as well as capital and technical assistance to agriculture and industry. Efforts to promote industrialization and to encourage the private sector likewise find their justification in their capacity to speed economic development. Prototypes of these programs are found in most of the projects of the World Bank and of the United States, in countries where economic development has become a major political issue. India is an example of a country whose aid projects, prior to the Chinese invasion of 1962, were essentially economic in their purpose.

The third group of aid tactics involves the effort to influence the direction of change, either by introducing reforms or by discouraging tendencies considered harmful to the purposes of the aid program. Some reforms (especially those in public administration) are intended to support or augment the economic development programs; others (such as land tenure and taxation) are aimed more generally at achieving social justice. There are also indirect political consequences of various technical reforms supported by foreign aid, but these are so unpredictable that they have seldom been considered a legitimate purpose of American foreign policy.

The United States has occasionally experimented with reform-inducing aid in countries where it had a special interest. In the Dominican Republic, for example, after the Trujillo dictatorship fell in 1961, American aid was consciously used to gain support for an acceptable interim government. American influence at first took the form of a series of impact projects to be announced by the leaders who seemed committed to democratically oriented development. A threatened withdrawal of U.S. aid followed when authoritarian tendencies appeared at the top. Still later, after Juan Bosch's government was elected to office, the United States continued the effort to maintain its influence through the use of aid. When that government in turn was overthrown in 1963, aid was suspended—not because economic growth was threatened, but because democracy had been sacrificed to the ambition of a military clique.[2] Again in 1965, U.S. aid was restored to prevent revolution, and it was offered in a way that would encourage political moderation. Other examples of deliberate efforts to influence political developments appeared in the sporadic offering and withholding of aid to President Diem in Vietnam, in the hope of influencing his internal politics.[3] Perhaps the closest approach to an official foreign aid doctrine of political change, however, is that formulated for the Alliance for Progress, which made political and social reform an element of the national development plan. One of the rare outbursts of optimism about foreign aid in the 1960's led to an effort to extend these reform principles on a worldwide basis.

None of these tactical approaches can contribute simultaneously to all of the United States objectives described in Chapter 1. The tactics leading to stability might produce authoritarian regimes with capricious foreign policies and unpleasant domestic politics; those contributing to economic development may introduce social injustice and encourage political instability; while those influencing the direction of change may interfere with economic productivity and develop or produce a backwash of reactionary protest. Programming aid for a country requires choices both in strategy and tactics.

TACTICS OF STABILITY

Except for relatively rare periods of national expansion, American diplomacy in the past century has attempted to maintain existing international relationships and power distributions. The fact that about one-third of United States foreign aid is presently military actually understates the American concern with security: much of the remaining aid is intended to provide enough economic strength to support national defenses against attack and subversion. Development means change.

---

[2] Abraham F. Lowenthal, "Foreign Aid as a Political Instrument: A Case Study of the Dominican Republic 1961-63," in *Public Policy*, ed. John D. Montgomery and Arthur Smithies (Cambridge: Harvard University, distributors, 1965), Vol. XIV.

[3] John D. Montgomery, *The Politics of Foreign Aid: American Experience in Southeast Asia* (New York: Praeger, 1962).

It may threaten the *status quo*. One of the primary purposes of foreign aid is to minimize dangers of war, insurgency, and revolution that might destroy or distort economic progress.

Both the *expanding* and the *maintaining* phases of international politics involve the underdeveloped countries. Many of them have been the victims of imperialism and after independence, the centers of unrest. A list of the international catastrophes of the postwar period, from Algeria to Zanzibar, would illustrate the reasons why the United States has applied foreign aid so intensely in the pursuit of stability. International stability seems to depend on internal stability although obviously the attempt to balance international military forces sometimes introduces domestic imbalances.

The most direct contributions to stability are those designed to prevent attack. Efforts to introduce a military deterrent in countries threatened by communism have clearly afforded some protection against outright invasion. Military unpreparedness, first in Korea and more recently in India, may well have encouraged the invasions of Korea in 1950 and India in 1962, just as military aid to Thailand and Pakistan appeared to stabilize those boundaries, at least momentarily. There are serious doubts about the long-term consequences of military deterrents, especially in underdeveloped countries, where regional rivalries may lead to war; but in the short run, military aid inspires confidence, and it can even permit national leaders to devote a larger share of available resources to developmental activities.

Other threats to stability posed by Communist power have been more difficult to counter. Conventional military strength does not offer much protection against subversion and guerrilla warfare. Foreign aid attempts to meet these forms of competitive coexistence by means of counterinsurgency efforts and support for police and military programs. Thus, local military forces receive aid in the form of special equipment and training for counterinsurgency in remote areas. More positive efforts seek to enlist local support against guerrillas by promoting rural development through the use of both civilian and military forces. Military units may join in with programs of Civic Action to help villagers build access roads, small dams and irrigation systems, schools, and other community facilities. These projects merge existing military engineering skills with local labor in the hope of improving the conditions of livelihood and morale among people otherwise considered highly vulnerable to Communist blandishments. If peasants can enjoy security while local improvements are being introduced, guerrilla action can be treated as a military problem.

Using military personnel to introduce rural reforms is at times a political gamble, however. The military context distorts normal diplomatic relations and political approaches to development. It gives the

Pentagon a preponderant influence in the designing and administration of country programs (in Vietnam, for example, the first American efforts to press the government for timely political reforms were discouraged by the U.S. Army's view that defections from the regime were a military problem). And from the host country's viewpoint, encouraging its army to participate in politics may weaken the chances of a stable regime (Vietnam also illustrates this danger: it was a military clique that unseated Diem and failed thereafter to restore stable rule). Sometimes, however, the civilian regime is unable to move fast enough to accommodate popular demands, and the military forces have to be used because they are the most modern and efficient agencies in the nation.[4]

Perhaps the most widespread criticism of military aid is that it diverts scarce funds from constructive developmental uses to uneconomic, unproductive activities. This objection is especially serious when investment capital is limited or the army is already extended beyond the apparent military requirements. In other situations, notably in Latin America, the national leadership sometimes requests military aid for prestige, and American responses to such appeals have the effect of promoting regional arms races.

In spite of these dangers, military aid will doubtless continue to be a major instrument of United States foreign policy. A military presence can repel an invasion before it starts; and the dispersal of military units throughout the countryside can also discourage communist infiltration and subversion in rural areas. Even for purely internal purposes, the army is sometimes the only well-integrated bureaucracy available to the central government's emergency or extraordinary programs, or for carrying out small-scale development projects such as dams, feeder roads, irrigation systems, schools, and civic centers. There have also been cases in which the army was the first agency to recognize the need for mobilizing the rural population and to volunteer leadership for such purposes. In both Burma and Pakistan, military intervention has served such needs.

It is also true that military aid has at times displaced other available forms of aid that might have produced more impressive economic results. But not all military aid is economically useless. Improvements in a nation's transportation and communication network are essential to military mobility and also contribute to economic development. Engineering activities of the military may likewise serve developmental objectives if the tasks themselves are well chosen (land clearing and the building of access roads, for example). Military service directly

---

[4] John J. Johnson, ed., *The Role of the Military in Underdeveloped Countries* (Princeton, N. J.: Princeton University, 1962), especially pp. 74 ff., 215 ff., and 286 ff.

contributes to the development of human resources by teaching trades and encouraging work habits and self-discipline. Military aid to such activities is not entirely misplaced even in terms of economic objectives; and other by-products of military aid, such as the construction of hospitals for the army's use and the encouragement of domestic suppliers of materiel in small industries and commercial enterprises, may also benefit the civilian economy.

The components of aid used to promote stability include supplying of materiel, military advice and training, operational assistance, and cash and commodity grants and loans in support of the economy. The organization necessary for these aid activities differs somewhat from country to country. Where large-scale advisory, training, or operational contingents of American troops are involved, something very like an American military camp may be established, complete with a formal chain of command, technical services and staff divisions, barracks, post exchanges, and military post-offices. But if only a few military experts are required to supervise procurement activities or offer technical advice, the organization may be small, informal, and almost completely merged with the corresponding agencies of the host government. In still other areas, where American aid supports a military dictatorship that is indifferent to development, there may be little more than a token national presence maintaining contact while awaiting more favorable political opportunities.

The activities considered necessary to create and maintain stability require more than a military buildup. Nearly all nations require adequate national armies and internal police agencies to establish minimum security conditions; but where social and political justice is ignored, political stability remains elusive. It is now well established that a sound economy is necessary not only to support the military effort itself [5] but, more importantly, to give the citizens, on whom an army depends, a stake in the order that they are expected to help defend.

TACTICS OF DEVELOPMENT AID

Development involves both increasing productivity in existing sectors where the technology is primitive, and diversifying the economy by introducing new products. Increasing productivity usually means working on the agricultural sector, a prospect that repels many politicians because it lacks glamour; and even if it is successful, it still leaves

[5] See Amos A. Jordan, *Foreign Aid and the Defense of Southeast Asia* (New York: Praeger, 1962); Harold A. Hovey, *U.S. Military Assistance, A Study of Policies and Practices* (New York: Praeger, 1965).

the nation in the position of supplier to more advanced nations. Diversifying the national product, on the other hand, often means industrialization and requires entrepreneurial skills and a commercial system that governments can rarely supply. In both cases, foreign aid may be used to supply technical knowledge, capital, and even manpower; but it can do little to overcome political obstacles such as indifference to agriculture or hostility to encouraging the private sector.

There are many reasons why concentrating on the agricultural sector is justified even apart from economics. Farming involves a vast majority of the population in the underdeveloped countries, and their loyalty is an important national asset (guerrilla activity is usually a rural, not urban, phenomenon). Agriculture may enable a dependent nation to feed its growing population better, though few underdeveloped countries have been able to increase their food production as rapidly as their population. (If present trends continue, in fact, many countries in Asia, Africa, and Latin America will face widespread famine during the 1970's.) The economic importance of the agricultural sector remains paramount, however. In the early years of development it provides a nation's principal source of capital for reinvestment and increases the scarce foreign exchange supply as products enter the export market or are used internally to replace products now being imported.

In spite of the urgency of modernizing the agricultural sector in most underdeveloped countries, the difficulties of doing so are staggering. Perhaps first among these are the technical problems: the impressive increases in agricultural productivity brought about in the United States cannot be immediately achieved in the tropical countries. Crop varieties that have produced immense yields in the United States have suffered in the tropics from unexpected diseases and pestilences, or have failed to respond because of different soil and climatic conditions. Lack of knowldge about these conditions has led to misuse of fertilizer and inadequate irrigation planning. Furthermore, ignorance of behavior patterns and social organizations of peasant farmers in many countries has made it difficult to find effective ways of gaining acceptance of new techniques even after they have been experimentally validated. In many situations, the agricultural extension worker's approach—a version of the county agent as teacher to the farmers—has failed to change the inefficient techniques and uneconomic practices of peasant communities. Even the community development approach, which seeks to mobilize local action to deal with "felt needs" at the village level, has sometimes met with indifference or produced activities irrelevant to agricultural output.

Apart from deficiencies in knowledge and approach, there are important political obstacles to making major improvements in the agricultural sector. Working with many farmers requires more human effort than negotiating with a few industrialists; education is a slower process than capital investment; and the urbanized political elites in the modern sector associate development with power lines and factories, not with field experiment stations and credit cooperatives. National plans therefore tend to overlook or downgrade the agricultural sector, whether in India, China, or even the Soviet Union, simply because the technicians who draw them up are less familiar with it than with the dramatic products of the industrial revolution. And even if the plans call for investment in irrigation and agricultural experimentation, it is difficult to inspire civil servants to work with farmers living in villages far from the amenities of the westernized major cities. The urban orientation of development administration is, of course, understandable in view of the obviously greater economic progress that is possible in an industrial society. Aid administrators, for their part, have often confirmed this preference for industry over agriculture in order to avoid creating competition for United States surplus farm commodities in the world market.

In spite of these difficulties, extensive aid to the agricultural sector has been rendered by the United States and bilateral agencies. Most United States aid missions have agricultural divisions with specialists in economics, education, and extension, and various technicians permanently assigned as advisers to the ministries concerned with rural development. The United Nations Food and Agricultural Organization also provides large-scale technical assistance in many parts of the world. Since the middle of 1965, all donor agencies have assigned high priority to increasing food production in the underdeveloped countries.

It is estimated that about half the anticipated increases in productivity will require the use of fertilizers, the other half taking place through the introduction of better seeds, more irrigation, better drainage, more pesticides, better agricultural implements, and better cultivation methods. Since multilateral activities have been largely confined to the second group of projects, the bilateral programs have had to offer most of aid required for building fertilizer plants. Such plants are costly, however, and if judged solely in terms of their immediate commercial prospects, not always profitable.

The second element of development aid involves the industrial sector, which is the most generally accepted road to modernization and product diversification. It also involves the greatest and most conspicuous capital outlay. Aid efforts to the agricultural sector amounted in 1963 and 1964 to less than 10 per cent of the American owned foreign currencies, and only one-fourth as much aid went to agriculture as to industry and mining.[6] The leaders of nearly every underdeveloped country are searching for ways of introducing industries that can absorb urban unemployment. They hope to produce goods that will reduce the need for imports and perhaps even enter into competition in the world market. Some seem to measure their achievements as statesmen by counting the number of smoking chimneys they can see on the skylines of the major cities.

Many political leaders in the underdeveloped countries distrust private enterprise as a means of industrialization. They associate capitalism with the colonial powers whose troops once came to capture and subdue. Whether it followed or preceded military adventures, the franc, pound, or dollar was foreign. It seemed to represent exploitation, loss of independence, and all other evils of imperialism. And experience with local capitalists has also been discouraging. Local captains of industry have included freebooters who did not hesitate to take advantage of loosely drawn laws or less enterprising competitors. Sometimes these merchants, like the Chinese in Southeast Asia and the Indians in East Africa, were second- and third-generation immigrants, and usually they were of low social status. Finally, from a religious viewpoint as well, many parts of the world consider the individual profit motive ignoble and unworthy, if not actually sinful. Ironically enough, it was the teachings of Marx, as absorbed by African and Asian leaders while students in foreign universities in the 1920's and 1930's, that gave political expression to these religious scruples about private profits. Many political leaders and civil servants consider capitalism a dirty word.

Hostility to private ownership, combined with the shortage of capitalistic managers and entrepreneurs, has often compelled foreign aid donors to choose between offering industrial assistance through the public sector or not at all. Sometimes the United States government has begun with aid to public corporations in order to speed industrialization, hoping that private enterprise would develop later. But this approach is uncertain, and it has encountered powerful political resistance in the United States. Support to a proposed publicly owned steel mill at Bokaro in India was successfully discouraged by the U.S. Congress in spite of efforts of the Kennedy administration to justify it. For while it is undeniable that industrialization breeds further industrialization, there is no assurance that such activity will encourage the private sector. Some governments seem committed to an indefinite

---

[6] AID, *Operations Report,* June 30, 1965. In 1965, project commitments in agriculture were $103.8 million; industry and mining, $258.15 million; transportation, $122.2 million; education, $61.4 million; and promotion of private enterprise, $75.2 million. On the other hand, there were about twice as many technicians engaged in "food and agriculture" as in "industry and mining." (AID, *Operations Report,* June 30, 1965.)

expansion of their activities in economic as well as social spheres, and United States policy is against contributing to such concentration of power.

Recognizing such difficulties, some critics of economic aid have argued that it ought to be discontinued on the ground that it actually discourages private enterprise and thus hinders development. This argument is based on the fact that aid is offered on a government-to-government basis and on the suspicion that aid promotes waste and encourages governments to relax their own efforts to raise capital by taxation and other forms of saving.[7] But the preponderance of evidence and opinion is that foreign aid has had the effect of stimulating and encouraging private enterprise in a number of countries. Moreover, new techniques for supporting private capitalism through foreign aid have also emerged.

The fact that aid is spent by governments rather than by private enterprises does not mean that the public sector is its sole, or even principal, beneficiary. On the contrary, public investments build dams that supply electricity to industry, and irrigation water for agriculture; public funds construct new highways that open up new markets, and schools that train manpower for commerce and industry. The largest share of economic aid supports "infrastructure" projects of this type, which directly benefit the private sector. As to the charge that aid promotes wasteful consumption rather than self-help through higher taxation and reinvestment, the evidence is less clear. Although certain forms of aid have indeed permitted the importation of luxury goods, they have also promoted private commercial activity and service industries. Contrary to popular impressions, "program" loans, which supply foreign exchange for commercial imports, represented 50 per cent of all development lending in the middle 1960's. They permitted the importing of capital equipment and raw material for industrial purposes, as well as consumer goods. It is doubtful that local tax rates have been lowered anywhere because of aid contributions to the national investment. Even in cases where foreign aid permitted the tax rates to remain stable, the result is an incentive to the private sector if economic policies are otherwise favorable. For these and other reasons, it is clear that American aid can be used to foster private enterprise, especially if it encourages favorable governmental policies among officials who might otherwise not recognize the private sector at all.

American aid to the private sector begins with the infrastructure projects, program or foreign exchange support, and efforts to encourage a favorable climate for attracting foreign investments and keeping

[7] These arguments are advanced by Milton Friedman in "Foreign Economic Aid Means and Objectives," *Yale Review,* Summer, 1958, and challenged by Charles Wolf, Jr. in "Economic Aid Reconsidered," *Yale Review,* Summer, 1961.

local money at home. In more recent years, it has included direct financing of industrial development and productivity centers (which offer consulting services and extend credit to industrial enterprises), as well as various industrial and agricultural banks, and geological, industrial, and market surveys commissioned to investigate the feasibility of various industrial proposals. A businessman's "Peace Corps" was organized in 1964 to provide managerial and technical skills for private enterprises. United States aid to the private sector usually operates through agencies and programs established by the host government. It is therefore dependent on (and can thus encourage) the existence of public attitudes and policies favorable to private enterprise.[8]

Other sources of aid to the private sector nevertheless still outweigh United States foreign aid efforts in both volume and versatility. Private investors, European governments, and the World Bank engage in similar activities, in some cases on a much larger scale than the United States. Large corporations are also investing large sums in commercial and industrial activities in the underdeveloped countries. Such acts are not always welcomed, however, especially in countries where foreign investments have become a political issue. United States private investments in Latin America, for example, rose to $540 million in 1959 but declined to somewhere between $90 million and $120 million in 1962, at least partly because of local hostility. Three-fifths of United States investment abroad has been in the high income countries where the risk is relatively small and the prospects of return favorable.[9] In an effort to reverse the trend against investment in the underdeveloped countries, American diplomacy has supported private capital ventures by negotiating tax and trade agreements, by bargaining for protection of United States owned property, by offering insurance against expropriations, and by guaranteeing various forms of international investment.

On the whole, however, foreign aid is a marginal influence in stimulating private development, both agricultural and industrial. It should be considered a means of accelerating change rather than of initiating it. Only a relatively small proportion of development requirements can be supplied from external sources. Foreign aid cannot provide the creative innovation and leadership needed to prepare a society for modernization. Even the capital requirements in most

[8] See Theodore Geiger and Winifred Armstrong, *The Development of African Enterprise* (Washington: National Planning Association, 1964), especially Chap. 5.
[9] Raymond F. Mikesell, ed., *U.S. Private and Government Investment Abroad* (Eugene: University of Oregon, 1962), pp. 6, 58-59. The extractive industries—mining, smelting, petroleum, and agriculture—have accounted for about two-thirds of the foreign investment in low income countries. For a discussion of British approaches see J. S. Forde, *An International Trade in Managerial Skills* (Oxford: Blackwell, 1957).

underdeveloped countries must be supplied largely (often 80 per cent or more) from internal savings and taxation.

Foreign aid can, however, significantly influence the direction and pace of development. By selecting from among several modernizing forces at work within a country, it can sometimes determine which of them is likely to prevail. The technicians, administrators, and entrepreneurs involved in the chosen sectors may well become the most influential among the modernizing elites in the economy.

An important tactic of development aid is, therefore, to exert its marginal influence selectively, when the alternative roads to modernization do not seem equally desirable. Modernization of the agricultural sector can take place, as the USSR demonstrates, through collectivization, but the results are economically less efficient than private, and sometimes smaller, holdings. And politically, as well, coercive controls over the farming sector are likely to produce dissatisfaction and instability, to inhibit human development, and possibly interfere with world marketing relationships. For these reasons, most United States aid efforts in agriculture have focused on services to individual peasant-cultivators. Similar considerations help to explain American preferences for widespread ownership in the industrial and commercial sectors. National planning and controls that are too detailed may produce economic distortions that are not responsive to market conditions or to cost factors. American policy is to support as large a private sector as the traffic will bear, in the belief that a mixed economy offers more diverse sources of power than a socialist state, and that this contributes to a pluralistic or democratic society. While such societies are in many ways harder to govern than a unitary or authoritarian society, they are less likely to fall prey to an irresponsible dictator or self-contained elite, and in turn, they are considered less likely to engage in foreign adventures that might threaten the security and peace of the region.

A developing society, being more complex than a traditional one, tends to increase the options open both to governments and their individual citizens. The nature and conduct of foreign aid programs in such societies may sometimes provide a decisive margin of influence in the critical choices that have to be made as modernization begins.

AID TACTICS FOR REFORM

Both internal stability and economic development may require changes in the political and administrative system in the host country and in its basic economic policies. The benefits of increased productivity must be well enough distributed to offer incentives to innovators and producers: this may call for a variety of reforms in tax and fiscal policy and land tenure. The masses must be able to see advantages in their own lives as a result of the new demands placed upon them: this may call for new social welfare policies and governmental attitudes toward the citizenry. New goods and services symbolic of modern society—mass education and consumers' goods, for example—must be available in quantities sufficient to maintain a continuous commitment to national goals: and this may mean deviations from capital development priorities. None of these decisions can be made easily, and the role of the external agent must therefore be played with great skill and sensitivity. Wherever the modern is emphasized, something traditional may have to be sacrificed.

It is now a truism to observe that the basic obstacles to growth are noneconomic. Illiteracy, lack of technical and managerial skills, social injustice, inadequate public administration, and vagueness of the national will cannot be eliminated by economic aid alone.

The use of aid to encourage reform involves a variety of tactics, ranging from building internal alliances with proponents of change to directly attacking obstacles to development. Insofar as reform means improvement in the conduct of public and private affairs, aid can provide skills and equipment to supplement local efforts. When changes in laws and institutions are necessary, foreign aid can support them by supplying consultants and institutional liaisons as well as various contract services. A third tactic is to require the performance of specific changes as a condition of aid. Or finally, a variety of pressures may be introduced to improve the standards of administrative performance by the host country. Whatever tactics are used, aid provides an avenue of communication and degree of attention that might not otherwise be available through diplomatic channels.

Supplying new knowledge as a means of introducing reform requires the use of technical assistants or experts in a variety of fields. They may be assigned to work with counterparts in the host government, either to supplement their knowledge or to assist local officials in carrying out projects supported by foreign aid. Where no counterparts are available, the visiting expert is assigned an operating role, working much as if he were a member of the host government's civil service. Either of these roles may afford an opportunity to recommend reforms necessary to the success of foreign projects. Usually such reforms are of a technical, and presumably nonpolitical, nature. Technicians may be supplied for these purposes as individuals or as members of a team, and from bilateral or international sources.

The second tactic of reform is associated with institution-building. It involves a deeper, and perhaps more permanent, penetration into the host society. If an institution is the "lengthened shadow of a man," the introduction of new laws and customs is an extension across time. When immediate project requirements begin to merge into long-term considerations of education and social change, certain self-sustaining forces of reform are set into motion. Institutions are also built to preserve and enlarge change introduced by technical advances. The most important of these institutions are engaged in education and research. Universities and teams of consultants brought under United States foreign aid contract have aided 37 institutes of public and business administration and economic planning throughout the underdeveloped world.[10] Other institution-building efforts include governmental reorganizations, development banks, and planning agencies that have been established (half-heartedly at first, perhaps) with the support of American funds.

Requiring the host government to make matching contributions, pass enabling legislation, or adopt administrative reforms as conditions of aid—the third tactic of reform—is closely related to the principle of self-help. Matching contributions increase the scope or dimensions of an aid operation by enlarging the resources available; they also increase the speed of development, by encouraging local initiatives. Even where these results are disappointing, the processes of giving aid, and of requiring better means of accounting and control, to insure that funds are used for their intended purposes, improve administrative capabilities and may thereafter extend to other governmental activities in the aid-receiving countries. The best example of this tactic is found in the Alliance for Progress. The original plans for the alliance envisioned a reciprocity of interest between the donor and users of aid funds, whereby essential social and political reforms would be undertaken as a condition of the exchange. Reforms were in fact introduced under this arrangement, but the American resoluteness in maintaining the momentum of reform has often slackened in the face of communist advances. The United States response to communism has been, all too often, to abandon reform efforts just as the demand for improvement is rising.

Negative sanctions and positive pressures represent the fourth and most drastic approaches to reform. They are the most drastic because they involve the donor power's taking responsibility. When one government rewards another for taking certain actions, it assumes a large measure of the risk in case of failure; and if it punishes another by withholding aid because of certain other actions, it risks defeating the purpose for which the aid was originally offered.[11] Assuming such risks requires a high degree of certainty about the development process and the possibility of manipulating it. Americans seldom feel such

[10] Hubert H. Humphrey, "Public Administration in the Developing Countries—the U.S. Approach," in *Public Administration—A Key to Development*, ed. Burton Baker (Washington: Graduate School of U.S. Dept. of Agriculture, April, 1964), p. 58.

[11] Montgomery, *Politics of Foreign Aid*, pp. 259-60.

assurance; but on a small scale, the tactics of reward and punishment have been effective. Massive uses are rare, however. Even in cases where a government rejects the proffered rewards and engages in actions hostile to American policy—as in Sukarno's Indonesia—the United States has hesitated to withdraw completely, because to do so would be self-defeating. For however strained the relations between donor and receiver of aid may be, foreign aid still serves the purpose of opening and protecting communications at both political and technical levels.[12]

Whenever developmental objectives require changes in current behavior and practice, it is to be expected that at least some of these tactics of reform will enter into the planning and administration of aid programs.

CONCLUSION: THE CONCEPT OF A COUNTRY STRATEGY

Perhaps the most disturbing aspect of the approaches described above is the implication that the donor nations conceive of some sort of political model toward which they are attempting to move the underdeveloped countries. Both parties to the aid relationship sometimes act as though this were the case: the donors, by attempting to impose conditions irrelevant to development needs or success in administering the aid project; and the recipient country, by showing resentment to even technical suggestions mildly offered, with no political overtones intended.

In spite of such aberrations and criticisms, however, no such models exist in the country aid programs. Western powers have found too many surprises in the developing areas to maintain very much confidence in their ability to predict— much less to control—their politics. And for their part, receiving countries can identify for themselves the reforms that are theoretically necessary to accomplish their developmental ends. Sometimes heads of state welcome external pressure to adopt reforms they consider necessary but hesitate to introduce on their own initiative. For reforms are nearly always unpopular with someone, and usually someone influential. In any case, attempting to impose one's own political or economic system upon other countries is both presumptuous and dangerous. Although the United States, the World Bank, and the Soviet Union all have strong preferences for supporting certain institutions of development, none of these are sufficiently systematic to resemble a model, and all have deviated from their own preferences when the alternatives seemed sensible.

[12] *Ibid.*, chaps. II, III.

If a model representing the goals of United States foreign aid exists at all, it is of a world order rather than in the details of nation-building. The desired direction of change, rather than its specific ends, informs most U.S. aid, whether undertaken bilaterally or through international organizations. The task of identifying and supporting desirable trends is a complex one. The desired goals are not the same for all countries; and sometimes two succeeding American Presidents, foreign aid administrators, or field directors have disagreed in planning programs for a single country.

The process of deciding on American objectives in a country requires plans, compromises, and negotiations. The Policy Planning Council of the Department of State prepares National Policy papers for each major country, representing a comprehensive general plan for American activities. More detailed planning papers are also prepared by each agency concerned: the State Department Guidelines, the Defense Department Internal Defense Plans and Long-Range Assistance Studies, the AID Country Assistance Program books and Long-Term Assistance Strategy Statements, the USIS Country Plans, and the Military Assistance Five-Year Plans are all examples of these. In March 1964, after nearly a year of experimentation, a Comprehensive Country Programming System (CCPS) was established to assist ambassadors in allocating resources to United States field activities in accordance with national objectives. This system also provided for additional staff to coordinate the planning in all elements of an American field mission. For the first time, means were provided to the ambassador to integrate the work of the political and economic sections of the Embassy, the United States AID Mission, the United States Information Service, the Peace Corps, the Military Assistance Staff, and the intelligence services. All of the techniques used in conducting international relations were incorporated in the system, as well as the more conventional diplomatic functions of reporting, rendering special services, and offering general support to the mission. According to the directions issued in the CCPS, the conduct of diplomacy at the country levels includes both efforts to influence (through official relations, contacts, exchanges, dissemination of information, and institutional relations) and the program of assistance (whether as loans, grants, guarantees, technical assistance, or credit sales). Efforts to coordinate field operations at the ambassadorial level are not, of course, new [13] and their impact on action in the country was small so long as CCPS referred only to staffing and coordination and not to the allocation of total available resources. But powerful instruments

[13] *The Ambassador and the Problems of Coordination. A Study Submitted by the Subcommittee on National Security Staffing and Operations to the Committee on Government Operations, U.S. Senate* (Washington: GPO, 1963).

for making such allocations were on the drawing boards. The greatest danger will lie in excessive reliance in Washington upon macro-economics and electronic computers in making decisions of diplomatic strategy in the use of aid resources.

Extending aid in the hope of promoting stability involves operations distinctly different from those aimed at development or reform. The kinds of tactics appropriate in inducing reform may appear in the short run to threaten stability, just as unquestioning support of apparently stable regimes may discourage reform efforts and permit the continuance of policies that inhibit development. A comprehensive view of the tactics appropriate to each of these purposes will help to explain why American policies have appeared in many cases to be unproductive and why United States funds have supported projects that conflict with American democratic or capitalistic preferences. For multiple goals are often incompatible: pursuing one or the other in turn leads to apparently aimless and contradictory tactics even though all of them are intended to serve the goals of American foreign policy. Therefore evaluating the successes and failures of strategic aid requires precise knowledge of the history of the goals and policies that led to each project.

4

Assessing Foreign Aid

Against expectations of the millenium, foreign aid must be counted a failure. Millenial claims continue to be made for it, however, along with equally extravagant challenges. Experts have told Congress that each foreign aid dollar buys nine or ten times as much military protection as the dollar spent on American troops. Congress is not so pleased, however, to learn that American-supported armies have helped to destroy the constitutions that they were organized to defend. If one witness claims that the Marshall Plan saved Europe, another charges the fall of China against foreign aid. A *New York Times* report suggested in 1964 that because Polish–American relations had deteriorated in the years after 1956, the U.S. had wasted its aid loans of $600 million in agricultural surplus commodities sent to that country; but in the same year, the AID Administrator noted that seventeen countries had made the transition from outside aid to economic self-support, predicting that fourteen other nations would soon be freed from dependence on extraordinary aid. In Cambodia (not one of the fourteen), Prince Sihanouk expressed his country's "eternal gratitude" for U.S. aid, a total of $725 million from 1953 to 1963, just as he ordered its termination as a protest against American policies in Southeast Asia. And Pakistan, among the largest beneficiaries of U.S. aid to the underdeveloped countries, became the anchor of two American alliances (CENTO and SEATO), but it still signed trade and commercial air agreements with Peking and created an embassy in Cuba (it was this action that led *Newsweek* to wonder how the U.S. "could plead the effectiveness of foreign aid in Congress"). The expectation that nations receiving U.S. aid ought to behave themselves received another blow a year later when Barrientos overthrew the Paz regime in Bolivia; the same magazine suggested that this signaled failure for the Alliance for Progress, because one of its "basic premises" was that "the combination of U.S. aid and homegrown social reform should produce peace, progress, and democracy." It concluded that "in Bolivia twelve years of such effort had not done so." [1]

If events have provided no dramatic affirmation of American foreign aid, expert judgments have offered little more unanimity. Barbara Ward (Lady Jackson) published an article entitled "Foreign Aid *Has* Succeeded," arguing that it had "begun to change the whole context within which the developing nations, the vast majority of mankind, look at the West and assess Western policies and intentions." [2] But former Ambassador Spruille Braden told a congressional hearing that foreign aid is "counter to our religion and our constitution. It encourages communism and foments collectivism and socialism all over the globe." [3] Professor Edward Banfield argued that "where cultural conditions are right for it, development will occur rapidly in the absence of any aid," adding, "no country is too poor to accumulate capital if its people are disposed to save and to invest, and the technical knowledge of the Western world is easily available to underdeveloped countries." [4] But Professors W.W. Rostow and Max Millikan were still enjoying something approaching official support for their view that "external capital will often make a critical difference between an upward spiral of economic, social and political development and a downward spiral of stagnation and decay," perhaps leading to a "take-off point" at which "sustained economic growth becomes possible." [5]

Even official views are contradictory. A $100 million earthquake relief program for the southern Andean region of Chile was severely criticized by the General Accounting Office for failing to follow the

[1] These two reports appeared respectively on Sept. 16, 1963, p. 38, and Nov. 16, 1964, p. 58.

[2] *The New York Times Magazine,* July 13, 1964, p. 19.

[3] Quoted, along with other criticisms, in Thomas S. Loeber, *Foreign Aid: Our Tragic Experiment* (New York: Norton, 1961), pp. 13-14.

[4] "American Foreign Aid Doctrines," in *Why Foreign Aid?* ed. Robert A. Goldwyn (Chicago: Rand McNally, 1962), pp. 12-13.

[5] *A Proposal: Key to an Effective Foreign Policy* (New York: Harper, 1957), especially p. 56.

original plan; but the Ambassador who reviewed the program was impressed by "the enormous task that had been accomplished."[6]

A closer examination of claimed achievements and failures of foreign aid is clearly called for.

CLAIMS AND COUNTERCLAIMS

The most presumptuous claims about foreign aid are those that attempt to evaluate it once and for all or on a global basis. Surely no program so vast can be credited with universal success or dismissed as a wholesale failure. On a case-by-case examination, both successes and failures can be documented. The earliest investigations of UNRRA in 1944, for example, showed evidence that the Soviet Union and East European Communists were using intenational aid funds for their own purposes in Poland, Yugoslavia, Albania, Czechoslovakia, Austria, and Romania.[7] On the basis of these charges, the U.S. Congress substituted more readily controllable bilateral forms of aid (see Chapter 2), which eliminated the political misuses of aid funds, especially for Communists' purposes. But millions of people were ready to testify their gratitude to UNRRA as a relief operation.

Issues of waste and inefficiency plagued foreign aid from the beginning. Critics found tractors rusting at ports during the 1940's, left by UNRRA because no arrangements had been made to move them where they were needed. A popular writer charged that the American International Cooperation Administration of the 1950's built a million-dollar dam where there was no water,[8] and newspapers described equally costly roads that were washed away because there was too much. Reports of projects that failed because of inadequate information, excessive haste, and errors of judgment have been gathered not only by newsmen but also by the "end use" audits of the Agency for International Development, itself, and by other inspections from Congress and the executive branch of the government. In AID alone, 1,600 full-time employees (including foreign nationals) are engaged in auditing and accounting, and 2,800 such investigations were carried out in 1964. These reports, together with

[6] *Annual Report of the Comptroller General of the U.S.* (Washington: Govt. Printing Office, 1964), pp. 208-10; *The New York Times*, Dec. 27, 1964.

[7] *Congressional Record*, LXXXXI, pp. 471, 7654, 8944, 8945, and elsewhere.

[8] Loeber, *Foreign Aid*, pp. 24, 25. The dam was a series of dikes built in Jordan to store rain water. Experimental dikes had captured enough water to produce excellent crops the first years, and additional dikes were built. The erratic weather produced no rain for the next five years, however (nearly nine-tenths of Jordan's land receives less than 200 mm of rainfall, in unpredictable quantities and location). Subsequent projects have brought some 15,000 acres under irrigation, but the dikes remained Nature's silent reproach of man.

those prepared by congressional staffs and other government auditing agencies, are extensively used by Congress and the press. Refuting such charges and justifying the decisions involved are much more difficult than criticizing them.[9] In any case, the result is that the public appetite for stories of governmental inefficiency is fed from both private and public sources.

Foreign aid successes have also been very well documented— all of the resources of AID are available to provide such evidence— but they have received scanty publicity (claims by an interested party are always suspect, especially if they concern foreign aid, dealing with faraway events and witnesses who, for the most part, have neither voting nor purchasing power). Each year a parade of statistics is presented before somewhat skeptical congressional committee members, who balance the record thereafter by introducing questions about facts that the agency left unmentioned. Perhaps the net effect is to emphasize more the difficulty than the achievement, but both are there for the public to examine.

The annual summaries presented to Congress by the AID agencies include statistics (in the Philippines, AID supplied paper and technicians to print more than 20 million textbooks) and results (in the Pacific coast region of Guatemala, a foreign aid project has almost eliminated malaria). Some of the projects' results are both dramatic and self-justifying: in one decade (1953-1962) India's cases of malaria dropped from more than 75 million to only 1,632, as a result of spraying, three-fourths of the cost of which—$206 million— was paid by the United States. Similar programs in Indonesia are equally dramatic, but they seem less self-justifying because of political doubts over the country's leadership: in 3 years, 58 million Indonesians were virtually freed fom the threat of malaria, but there was no assurance that they might not be used as Sukarno's guerrilla fighters against Malaysia. Some of the achievements reported to Congress are uninterpreted quantities, like the 1,375,000 Iranian peasants who were taught farming, home economics, and sanitation by agricultural workers who, in turn, had been "trained by AID specialists." Some of the reported statistics are puzzling: the 1,300 chicks and 2 incubators imported to Eastern Nigeria with AID funds appear trivial unless the reader is able to envisage the subsequent rise of some 200 prosperous new poultry enterprises in the region. Sometimes the reports seem designed to appeal to domestic considerations without regard to their overseas impact: the fact that $119.7 million had been issued in guarantees protecting U.S. private investment in Argentina in fiscal year 1965; or that in 1963, U.S. vessels carried 5.3 mil-

[9] John D. Montgomery, *The Politics of Foreign Aid: American Experience in Southeast Asia* (New York: Praeger, 1962), Chap. IV and App. III.

lion tons of cargo shipped by AID—81 per cent of the total of foreign aid shipments, as opposed to 59 per cent in fiscal year 1961; or that $855 million worth of aid goods—78 per cent of all aid-financed commodities—were purchased in the U.S., regardless of price, compared to less than 50 per cent in 1958 when worldwide competitive bidding was in force.

Describing the accomplishments of foreign aid in terms of hundreds of rivers and streams dammed, thousands of miles of roads built, tens of thousands of schoolrooms in operation, hundreds of thousands of literacy classes conducted, or millions of people vaccinated will not satisfy critics of the costly foreign aid operations. The issue is not what American dollars have *bought* but what they have *done*. Dams, schoolrooms, classes, and the improvement of public health are only means of approaching the basic objectives of American foreign policy.

Measuring the short-term accomplishments of American aid is deceptively simple. When aid is used for humanitarian purposes, for example, its value is already achieved when relief is rendered to those in need. When symbolic gifts are presented, their end is served if they are accepted in evidence of American good will, power, or prestige. If services such as the use of a base or other military advantages have been exchanged for American gifts, the only issue is whether a reasonable bargain was driven. Nobody questions the fact that diplomatic gifts have served such purposes.

Major questions are left, however: whether U.S. aid has contributed to a just, peaceful, and prosperous world in some quarters or weakened the communist appeal in others; whether friendly nations that show prospects of economic growth or political or social maturity have been able to develop further along lines considered favorable; whether U.S. foreign aid has strengthened its position and that of the free world, or advanced its basic values, or protected the vital interests of its allies.

The difficulties in attempting to evaluate these long-term achievements are several: few of them are ever permanently attained; no single factor causes major political events to happen, and the relative importance of U.S. foreign aid in achieving desired results cannot often be measured. Sometimes the original objectives were incorrectly chosen, obscurely stated, or subsequently changed. Finally, quite apart from these theoretical considerations, even if the end consequences of foreign aid could be clearly and unmistakably traced, it would still not be possible to set a price upon many of them. How much was it worth to keep South Vietnam out of communist hands for a decade, or to insure Taiwan's freedom after the fall of mainland China? What is the financial value to America of a prosperous, reasonably united Europe, or a reconstructed Japan able to support United Nations actions in Korea? How much does it matter to the United States whether African states that are not yet economically viable are given the means of remaining outside the Iron Curtain? What price a Burmese neutrality as opposed to its possible incorporation into China? Can a value be attached to the continued independence of countries where the fact or prospect of dictatorship or oppression remain?

It is clear that success in foreign aid is likely to appear unpredictable, transitory, and perhaps even accidental, unless evaluated carefully.

LEVELS OF SUCCESS

The government cannot avoid making some assessment of foreign aid, however difficult the task may be. Questionable domestic programs are often continued simply because of the political support they generate. They can therefore survive years or even decades of ineffectiveness. Other public activities are accepted as traditional obligations of statehood and thus flourish even if they develop no constituency or are conducted outside the public view. But foreign aid has none of these advantages: it enjoys neither an important domestic following nor the sanction of custom, and its misdeeds are exposed both abroad and at home. Even those who believe that a state's actions should be dictated out of humanitarianism would not have to support the present complex economic and political rationale of foreign aid: a simple sharing of food and other necessities might serve this obligation. Both a consideration of the extent to which foreign aid actually serves the objectives established for it and an appraisal of its unintended other effects are necessary.

Judgments of this sort can be made at four operating levels: in appraising the performance of *individual* technicians, in evaluating *projects* or functional activities, in reviewing *country* programs, and in considering *regional* or other international effects. Judgments at each of these levels of evaluation can be made independently of the others: a successful technician may embark on a project that fails; in every country program that seems to go sour, one can find some redeeming project activity; within regions that are wracked by disorder or stagnation, sometimes impressive achievements are found. There seem to be as many criteria of success as there are technicians or projects or country programs or regions—or evaluators. Yet for practical purposes, comparisons must be made: technicians have to be promoted or transferred or released; projects have to be renewed, enlarged, reduced, or terminated; country aid levels have to be fixed in accordance with the evidence and prospects of success as well as the donor's national concern; regional efforts, at present only in a tentative exploratory stage, must compete for support with country programs whose pay-off is much more readily visible. Neither critic, advocate, nor practitioner of foreign aid can escape the necessity for evaluation.

Technicians

Measuring the performance of individual technicians involves both administrative and psychological considerations, with relatively little attention to the larger issues of national policy. One of the most discouraging discoveries in recent studies of employee ratings in technical assistance has been the fact that no two raters agree very substantially either on what elements are important to success or on how well individual technicians have performed. The only large-scale analysis of the components for success in overseas administration has emerged with a list of factors resting largely on judgment rather than on empirical evidence, and even these factors cannot be measured objectively.[10] Several careful appraisals of success ratings prepared by different observers of the same people— ratings made by the supervisor, a colleague, and the person himself— suggest that "success" usually lies in the eye of the beholder rather than in any objective factor.[11] It is possible that some kind of composite evaluation could be devised, using weighted ratings compiled into a single index, but this operation would be both complicated and costly and would still leave unsettled the question of finding adequate criteria.[12] A better hope for objectivity would lie in obtaining factual accomplishments as a basis of the assessment, with details supplied by the individual, his counterparts, his colleagues, and his supervisor, including claimed achievements, obstacles to greater success, and other results. Such indices might not result in creating a

[10] Harlan Cleveland, Gerald J. Mangone, and John Clarke Adams, *The Overseas Americans* (New York: McGraw-Hill, 1960). The factors identified in this subject are plausible and potentially useful to recruiters even though they are hard to identify. They are technical skill, belief in mission, cultural empathy, sense of politics, and organizational ability.

[11] Hollis Peter and Lawrence Schlesinger, *Using U.S. Training in the Philippines: A Follow-up Survey of Participants* (Washington: ICA; Ann Arbor: Institute for Social Relations of the University of Michigan, 1959). This survey actually applies to native technicians rather than foreign technical assistants. Leonard Goodwin, *American Professors in Asia, A Study of the Selection and Adaptation of 50 American Professors under the Fulbright-Hays Program* (Washington: Dept. of State Policy Review and Research Staff, June, 1964), esp. Part III.

[12] Hollis W. Peter and Edwin R. Henry, "Measuring Successful Performance Overseas," *International Development Review*, III, No. 3 (October, 1961).

numerical index of success, but they would contribute to developing criteria of achievement that would minimize the role of personal tastes and preferences. They would also help to develop a better understanding of the nature of the task and the wide variety of situations in which it must be performed.

Projects

Projects are usually measured in terms of technical or professional criteria. But such criteria may be somewhat shallow in terms of U.S. objectives. The malaria eradication project in Latin America, mentioned above, involved spraying 10 million homes with DDT in 1963; it offered protection to 59 million people, while another 44 million persons were being protected by programs of surveillance in areas where malaria had been effectively eliminated. These figures reveal an intensive effort, but further analysis is necessary to measure its final results. In some cases, economic standards could be applied: in the Pacific coast region of Guatemala, where foreign aid helped eliminate the threat of malaria, new lands were brought under cultivation, with the result that the agricultural income of the area increased 60 times between 1957 and 1962.

The economic value of project activities is sometimes very difficult to measure, however. Projects in agriculture can sometimes be analyzed by comparing their immediate impact on productivity with their total cost; yet increases or decreases in crop yields may be caused by nature rather than by man. It is sometimes assumed that over a period of time these effects of nature roughly cancel each other out, but this may not be true if soil and water are being depleted. It is also possible to calculate the increased productivity that results from improvements in public health.[13] More subtle calculations have been made to show the economic value of education and to impute a share of that value to foreign aid in proportion to its contribution to the expansion of educational facilities.[14]

---

[13] It is sometimes argued that the underdeveloped countries are plagued by disguised unemployment (i.e., workers are engaged in relatively unproductive tasks, or they are seasonally idle) and therefore do not gain economically from improved health in the work force. This argument is still undemonstrated. (See Theodore W. Schultz, "The Role of Government in Promoting Economic Growth," in *State of the Social Sciences,* ed. Leonard D. White, Chicago: University of Chicago, 1956; and R. S. Eckaus, "Factor Proportions in Underdeveloped Areas," *American Economic Review,* XLV, September, 1955.) Regardless of the merits of this argument, if new capital and technology are being introduced to increase productivity, improvements in the health of workers might amplify the increases.

[14] Cf. Frederick Harbison and Charles Meyers, *Education, Manpower, and Economic Growth* (New York: McGraw-Hill, 1964); and R. S. Eckaus, "Economic Criteria for Education and Training," *Review of Economics and Statistics,* XLVI, No. 2 (May, 1964), pp. 181-90.

Economic analysis used in such ways provides one measure of the relative value of different projects and serves as a guide to further investment of foreign aid funds. But it does not take into account the degree of difficulty encountered in different situations (a small gain in Pakistan agricultural productivity might have been more difficult to achieve than a large one in Japan), and it ignores the fact that much foreign aid is not necessarily an investment that can be placed in order to get the greatest economic return (in the 1960's, for example, it might be more important to make small gains in Indian agriculture than to make large ones in Israel).

Evaluating project achievements may also involve exercising professional judgments about their long-term capacity to influence the direction and speed of the modernization process. Philip M. Glick and Arthur T. Mosher appraised various aspects of American technical assistance in agriculture, analyzed administrative and organizational approaches of agricultural projects in Latin America, evaluated their impact on agricultural practices, and judged their effect on governmental farm programs.[15] Different approaches to technical assistance and to agricultural research and extension all came in for close scrutiny and criticism, largely based on professional standards, subjective observations, and the opinions of the principal participants in the programs. It is noteworthy that although both of these evaluations report favorably on the administrative arrangements that prevailed in the Latin American program, a decision was reached in Washington a few years later to terminate these special organizations (known as *servicios*) and convert all operations to the more conventional bilateral relationship. The decision to withdraw from a form of foreign aid considered a technical success was evidently based on entirely different standards than those prevailing in the field. As is often the case, Washington was inclined to favor criteria established by government financial auditors who suspected the *servicios* of loose accounting practices and a blurred responsibility between U.S. and Latin American members; and they feared that the U.S. might be committing itself to an endless task.

If agricultural projects present a variety of possible approaches in evaluation, even greater difficulties are encountered in fields that only indirectly affect productivity, such as public administration. It has been argued that aid in public administration was offered rather half-heartedly in the first place, because of reluctance to enter so intimately into the affairs of other governments. Even where such aid

---

[15] Philip M. Glick, *The Administration of Technical Assistance: Growth in the Americas* (Chicago: University of Chicago, 1957), and Arthur T. Mosher, *Technical Cooperation in Latin American Agriculture* (Chicago: University of Chicago, 1957).

was requested, it was not always vigorously administered because American and UN officials often harbored doubts about the "state of the art" of public administration and its transferability from one setting to another. Projects have nevertheless been established to assist governments in planning, building, and organizing their present functions and the new developmental ones. Other public administration projects have provided educational assistance to training institutes and to individual officials, while a third group of projects in public administration has supplied manpower to demonstrate techniques or actually to administer activities of government.

Evaluating public administration projects may thus require appraising their effects both on governments (civil service laws or regulations adopted, new budgeting and accounting procedures in use, or reorganizations carried out) and on programs (censuses taken, individual civil servants trained, or institutes established). In evaluating its own public administration accomplishments for fiscal year 1962, for example, the Agency for International Development reported that it had committed $19.5 million to 123 projects in 57 countries (largely in Africa and Latin America). The accomplishments were listed in quantitative terms where possible: 716 people were brought to the United States or other countries for training; a census in Thailand was completed in 2 years instead of 6 years, as in the previous (1947) census; 5,000 government officials in Thailand were given in-service training in an Institute of Public Administration established with U.S. aid; in Afghanistan, a budget system was established that could render accounts within 10 days after each period instead of 2 years, required by the previous system; new fiscal and control procedures in Paraguay's customs and tariff department increased total government revenues nearly 22 per cent without any change in the rate structure. But some equally important achievements lacked any quantitative description: a new budget law and budget bureau were established in Thailand, and a new statistical service in Iran distinguished itself by discovering previous errors that had underestimated the gross national product by one-third while doubling the cost of living estimates on which many governmental contracts were based. Sometimes the consequences of public administration projects could not be identified at all, including indirect effects such as the organizational ideas that did not take root until years after the originating technicians had left them behind, or the changed attitudes toward efficiency and honesty that may have developed out of tours of other nations or casual observation and untraceable new insights. What evaluation means in such cases is the exercise of professional judgment, augmented by as much evidence as field research can gather.

The difficulty of evaluating foreign aid projects should counsel caution, not despair. Most results of project operations can be identified by carefully conducted opinion surveys, quantitative analysis, and historical studies. But such evaluations are seldom available through official channels.[16] They are costly, and therefore must be selective. Because they may touch sensitive nerves, they may have to be conducted with discretion and usually by disinterested outsiders (sometimes by institutions like universities or foundations that can assemble teams of scholars to engage in field evaluations). Only a small sample can be thoroughly evaluated (the cost of studying the 2,700 aid projects underway in 1966 would equal another aid program in itself). And finally, because their purpose, approaches, and problems are all different, it is likely that different methods of evaluation will be necessary for various types of projects. By the mid 1960's, the Agency for International Development and private foundations had begun serious efforts to make project assessments and to support research and evaluation activity by individual social scientists and by universities and other institutions.

The importance of evaluating projects in terms of their impact on an entire sector of the society has recently emerged as a matter of doctrine in the Agency for International Development. In 1965, the agency undertook a careful study of the possible uses of evaluation as a management tool. After exploring AID's own resources and experience, a special committee concluded that the natural center of gravity for evaluation was the country mission. But evaluation was to be more than a mere programming exercise or a series of introspective project histories: it was to go beyond each project and into its sector (agriculture, education, or public health, for example). The purpose was to get at the interrelationships among project activities (why build schools, for example, if no teachers were available? and why train teachers for fields in which there are no students or no demands?).

One may question whether even this broadened view would be enough. A thoroughgoing country evaluation process would have to transcend both the project and the sector, looking to the society as a whole to appraise the impact of development activities (a dam may increase agricultural productivity through irrigation, for example;

---

[16] Access to official channels is, however, essential in a thoroughgoing evaluation of projects or functional activities. Much of the usefulness of Edward W. Weidner's extensive survey of public administration activities was possible because of access to project reports, his freedom to interview participating officials, and other courtesies extended by the cooperating agencies. (*Technical Assistance in Public Administration Overseas: The Case for Development Administration.* (Chicago: Public Administration Service, 1964.) Cf., for a project evaluation in business administration, Walter H. Carpenter and Charles L. Webster, "Communicating Business Ideas to Europe—A Case Study," *Journal of Business,* XXVIII, No. 3 (July, 1955).

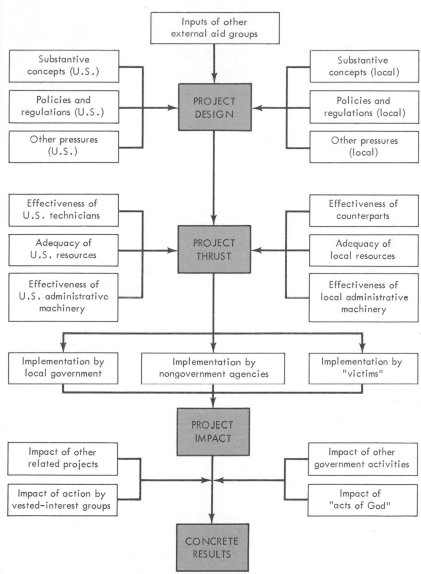

Courtesy of Paul A. Schwarz, American Institutes for Research.

but if people are forced to move out of the path of a storage reservoir or if public health is threatened by bilharziasis or malaria along the irrigation channels, then social welfare and public health specialists as well as engineers ought to participate in the evaluation). Wisdom seems to dictate that such evaluation should begin at the project level, where the impact is most direct, but that the success or failure of a project should be considered as well in terms of consequences that extend far beyond its original purposes.

Country Programs

Country programs are reviewed for both their economic and political impact. Successes are most readily demonstrated over a long span of time, especially where the economic standard of self-sustaining growth is applied. Failures, on the other hand, are immediately apparent, especially if they are political. According to official statements, the U.S. economic objectives were achieved in the countries of Marshall Plan Europe months ahead of schedule and at a cost of billions of dollars less than had been allocated. But in Cuba, the United States so completely lost the hope of achieving its objectives that it withdrew in despair. The forces that may bring about economic progress seem to be more predictable and measurable than those involved in political change, which often appears to be capricious and transitory.

The intractable nature of political development is one of several reasons why U.S. policy has been to avoid aiding it officially. As Chapter 3 has already suggested, however, American long-term strategy postulates that U.S. political interests are served by supporting sound economic development in many countries.

Official reports of country aid programs emphasize economic achievements first of all, followed by scattered references to projects that have contributed to them. Political claims for foreign aid, even those of stability, are less frequently encountered, partly because the achievements themselves are so fragile that they might be shattered by an unexpected coup the day after the report was issued. In any case, the role of foreign aid in introducing and supporting favorable political development is seldom clear; and even where American support has been a mainstay to a regime or a movement, it is often shortsighted to assert this fact and risk the political consequences that could predictably follow both at home and abroad.

Economic progress in Western Europe resulted in a termination of nearly all Marshall Plan aid by fiscal year 1963: to Sweden and Ireland as early as 1952; to Belgium, Luxemburg, West Germany, and Denmark in 1954; to the Netherlands in 1955; Portugal in 1957;

Norway in 1958; and Austria, France, Italy, and the United Kingdom in 1959; to Iceland in 1961; Spain in 1962; and Yugoslavia in 1963. But in 1964, Poland was still receiving U.S. aid (under a special congressional authorization for a children's hospital in Krakow); Greece was receiving development loans; and Turkey continued to receive aid partly because of its military requirements under a treaty of alliance with the United States.

The phasing out of economic aid to Europe was possible because of extremely favorable conditions for reconstruction. But of the 80-odd countries and territories receiving U.S. aid in 1964, only about 14 (including Greece, Taiwan, and Israel) were thought to be nearing the point at which soft loans and grants would no longer be necessary.[17] At the opposite end of the spectrum was a group of about 40 countries where U.S. objectives were limited to traditional diplomatic roles (such as establishing a presence) or to offering an exchange for base rights or other favors. By 1965 all 54 or so of these programs combined amounted to only about 12 per cent of the total aid allocation. Most American aid was addressed to about 25 countries where the objectives were hopefully *change-oriented*. These are the situations in which the achievements of American aid are most difficult—and most important—to weigh.

Perhaps 7 of the 25 or so major change-oriented country programs were addressed primarily to economic development, and nearly half of the total AID budget in 1965 was assigned to them. In these countries (India, Pakistan, Turkey, Chile, Colombia—later replaced by Brazil, Nigeria, and Tunisia) the economic prospects were considered good, but the speed of American withdrawal would depend as much on military and diplomatic developments as on the efficiency with which aid capital was used. In another 11 countries (mostly in Latin America), American interests were substantial, but the capacity to use aid effectively was limited. In contrast to the first group of change-oriented programs, in this group a measure of success of American aid would be short-term *increases* in the total amount offered. Increases would presumably reflect greater capacity to absorb development funds, and the transition from soft to commercially feasible hard terms would be expected to follow. Such a transition would indicate improvement in political and administrative conditions favorable to economic growth; and it is for this reason that in efforts such as the Alliance for Progess, the U.S. was exerting its influence to encourage a variety of reforms.

The last group of change-oriented countries, perhaps 7 in number, was still threatened by communist invasion or subversion or

---

[17] Because these categories are not fixed, only approximate numbers will be given for each of them.

various forms of internal instability. These nations (Laos, Vietnam, the Congo, Jordan, Korea, Bolivia, and Thailand) required aid for their very survival. Because their independence or national integrity was still in doubt, there was little prospect either for the economic growth that would permit American withdrawal or for reforms and administrative improvements favorable to further development. Measuring the effectiveness of aid to these countries would involve an appraisal of changes in military security and political stability, and of the part played in them by friendly external forces. The most celebrated cases of success in this regard are in the Greek–Turkey program that began in 1947 (although in the case of Greece the success in countering insurgency may have been as much because of Tito's change of politics as because of the counterinsurgency activities supported by American aid.) [18] The Philippines produced later evidence that programs of this type are not hopeless. The greatest discouragements are expressed, as of the middle 1960's, for the Congo and the former states of Indochina. As one correspondent pointed out just after the fall of the Paz government in Bolivia, reflecting over similar coups in Argentina and the Dominican Republic, "Neither U.S. aid nor its accompanying political leverage is enough to save constitutional government from military coups." [19]

Regional Programs

Regional aid programs usually represent approaches to objectives that individually negotiating countries would find impossible, distasteful, unnecessary, or politically hazardous to undertake. Thus, for example, the Mekong River Development project secured the cooperation of Laos, Cambodia, Vietnam, and Thailand in a common effort that none could have undertaken alone; in fact, some of these countries had broken off diplomatic relations with each other.[20] Similarly, under the Alliance for Progress, nations of the Western Hemisphere in planning development operations can cooperatively establish economic and technical standards that would be difficult for any one of them to adopt alone or to urge upon others. And in East Africa, American aid supported higher education on a regional

[18] See Brown and Opie, *American Foreign Assistance* and U.S. Dept. of State, "Assistance to Greece and Turkey," *Quarterly Reports to the Congress* (Washington: Govt. Printing Office, Sept. 30, 1947-June 30, 1949), Nos. 1-8. See also William Hardy McNeill, *Greece: American Aid in Action, 1947-1956* (New York: The Twentieth Century Fund, 1957).

[19] Henry Raymont, *The New York Times*, Nov. 22, 1964. Cf. Abraham F. Lowenthal, "Foreign Aid as a Political Instrument: A Case Study of the Dominican Republic 1961-63," in *Public Policy*, ed. John D. Montgomery and Arthur Smithies (Cambridge: Harvard University, distributors, 1965), Vol. XIV.

[20] C. Hart Schaff and Russell H. Fifield, *The Lower Mekong Project* (Princeton, N. J.: Van Nostrand, 1963).

basis, with selected universities establishing or enlarging professional schools so that each could serve a group of countries and perhaps achieve important economies of scale. This scheme introduced forms of cooperation and specialization that would have been difficult for the separate ministers of education to achieve. In such regional programs, it might be possible to identify the economic benefits of individual projects, but these would be only symbols of the international objectives of regionalism in aid operations. As is often the case with remote or hazy objectives, progress toward the goals of regionalism often seems imperceptible.

The most ambitious regional program of U.S. aid in the 1960's was undertaken through the Alliance for Progress—ambitious not in financial terms (the Asian programs have been larger, though declining), but in the scope it offered to cooperative planning, its delegation of authority to an independent council of experts, and the extent of its commitment to long-term social and economic change. America's participation in the Alliance for Progress is linked to a Latin American development charter signed at Punta del Este, Uruguay, in 1961, in which the twenty signatories undertook to provide about $100 billion in investment funds over a ten-year period. The American pledge to provide $20 billion of that included both public and private resources (the fiscal year 1965 AID commitment was $512 million, mostly in the form of development loans), but 80 per cent of the total was to come from the Latin American countries themselves. The concept of both supplying and jointly applying these funds was a greater commitment to regionalism than any development operations since the creation of the Organization of European Economic Cooperation under the Marshall Plan. The regional projects established with U.S. aid, for example, included the organization of several hundred credit unions, a training program conducted by the Latin American Tax Advisory Reserve, a variety of leadership training programs, a textbook production center, loans for industrial development on a regional basis in Central America and Panama, and provision of grant aid to the Central American economic community. The effort to encourage careful planning for development purposes led six countries—Bolivia, Chile, Colombia, Honduras, Mexico, and Venezuela—to submit development plans to an organization of American States Economic Panel for review. Cooperative effort to increase governmental revenues resulted in reported improvements in the tax programs of 16 countries, in many cases accompanied by significant increases in collections. Regional programs may not be impressive in terms of size or physical facilities, since the activities of individual states are their primary achievements.

Evaluating regional programs is not, then, merely a matter of measuring costs and benefits. Regional efforts may be essentially diplomatic; regionalism in aid is a method, not a program, and the mere existence of useful projects may be its best justification. There are, it is true, symbolic projects whose value can be estimated in the same manner as any other projects. But the regional effort is essentially an approach to cooperation that might not otherwise be forthcoming. If regional cooperation is considered a means of preventing catastrophe in Algeria or minimizing the threat of subversion from Cuba, American support is certain to continue. Even if regional designs in the Middle East, for example, do not bring together the lions and the lambs in Egypt and Israel, the effort is likely to be charged to diplomatic overhead rather than abandoned as a failure.

CONCLUSION

The elements of possible success in foreign aid may be classified according to purposes even if they cannot always be precisely measured. For present purposes, the classification suggested in Chapter 1 will be followed.

Most observers would identify *diplomatic* success in aid programs that succeeded in opening or maintaining dialogue with a regime not otherwise engaged in meaningful negotiations with the United States. In other cases, aid may help to create a favorable public opinion of the United States and enhance receptivity to American diplomatic objectives or other national purposes. Specific projects may be hailed by sectors of the American public that have benefited economically in terms of their overseas interests and investments. Finally, the national interest is clearly advanced where useful concessions overseas—military or otherwise—are maintained by means of *compensatory* foreign aid.

Strategic success is often measured in terms of the rate and direction of modernization. Foreign aid projects can introduce and support technical innovations that can be clearly identified and traced. In purely economic terms, project success can also be directly measured as productivity increases, and as output is diversified and improved. Other economic measures include lowered costs (reflected in profits, wages, and price reductions) and improvements in the export–import balance. An indirect measure of foreign aid productivity is the increased foreign and domestic investment that results from improvement in the economic climate.

Where the strategic aims are political, achievements in aid are often considered in cold-war terms: a stabilized international position of the U.S. and its allies, or an improved internal capacity to resist insurgency and domestic dissidence. But political achievements may also be identified in absolute terms related to the requirements of modernization. These dimensions include the introduction of government policy favorable to economic and technical improvement and increased administrative capacity to support the processes of change. Finally, political achievements may be reflected in improved social policies leading to better distribution of wealth, enhanced perception of the demands of social justice, and even, sometimes, improvements in the government's capacity to change its leadership in accordance with popular demand.

Success scores are not necessarily in measurable units, but they reflect the range of potential achievement in foreign aid. They are the most frequently identified items among the aspirations of American foreign aid policy beyond those of immediate national security and economic interests. But they are not interchangeable: charges of failure in any one category—diplomatic, technical and economic, or political—cannot be laid against the program as a whole unless results in the others are also negligible or unfavorable.

However one may appraise the successes and failures of American aid, the alternatives to continuing some form of aid are almost unthinkable. If the past could be relived, assuming that the United States had not offered foreign aid, could Germany and Japan have been left to reconstruct themselves under the permanent restrictions that would have been necessary to prevent the return of militarism? Would the European economies have recovered from their deep depression with no assistance from the United States other than the restoration of normal trade relations? Could the Common Market have come about by the initiative of European statesmen in the competitive national revival? Could the U.S. have ignored the postwar colonial independence movements but still have helped noncommunist leaders develop plans for the colonies, postwar modernization and growth and then secure the capital and skills to carry them out? It is possible to imagine such a world and its consequences for the U.S., just as it is possible to conceive of a renewed American isolation along traditional, prewar lines. But to imagine such a world is almost surely to reject it.

Even an intermediate form of action between total isolation and the present scale of U.S. involvement would not seem desirable to most citizens. It is likely that the U.S. could have engaged in other diplomatic activities to avoid the worst consequences of total isolation. Foreign aid could conceivably have been terminated with the military governments of Germany and Japan and the Marshall Plan, if the United States had ignored the developing countries as nations of relatively small economic or diplomatic importance and even less military power in world politics. But this calculation dismisses not only moral considerations and diplomatic realities, but also certain power factors that are inescapable in the nuclear age. Unrest and instability in any part of the world may threaten vital interests and possibly the immediate security of the United States. Even where the U.S. has no commercial, military, or cultural interests, the overthrow of regimes, the civil war of classes or groups contending for what advantages there are in the underdeveloped countries, and widespread dissatisfaction with the present order invite intervention by Communist forces. Once this has occurred, calculations of the immediate interests of the U.S. and its allies threaten to provoke Western or American involvement at a more serious level, and such escalation might lead to a confrontation of the great nuclear powers. Foreign aid does not necessarily prevent this from happening: China, Laos, and Vietnam illustrate that even large aid programs may not be enough to prevent the erosion of public support, possible Communist exploitation and agitation, and eventual confrontations on the brink of major war. But there are many places where, with American aid, the existing regime or a reform regime was able to satisfy public demands, demonstrate reasonable progress, and contain political differences within a framework of laws and constitutions.

An examination of the technical successes claimed by foreign aid spokesmen is, therefore, only a beginning of the evaluation of aid. A more serious approach to the problem of foreign aid is to consider means of improving its prospects for success.

5

Trends and Prospects

Even after two decades and sixty billion dollars, foreign aid gives the impression of precocious adolescence. In its purposes, administration, and theory, it has undergone almost constant change. A cynic might find nothing permanent in it except unsolved problems.

Changes in American foreign aid have resulted as much from domestic factors in the United States as from currents in world politics or advances in the sciences and arts of development administration. The major problem in American overseas operations is still to create and preserve continuity of support at home while remaining flexible enough to respond to the changing needs and opportunities abroad. This is not to say that all foreign aid problems would be resolved if stable political support were forthcoming; more knowledge about the development processes and the art of intercultural administration is also necessary. But these two issues are related: public and congressional attacks on foreign aid have repeatedly forced the agencies involved to reorganize, just when they were achieving self-confidence and beginning to support the research needed to generate further improvements. Foreign aid suffers from an irresistible, popular tendency to pull the plant up to see if its roots are growing. This chronic rootlessness increases its vulnerability to political accident. Understandably, the resultant changes in foreign aid operations have not always been improvements.

RECENT TRENDS IN AMERICAN AID POLICIES

In spite of its uncertainty of tenure, foreign aid has not been static. Major recent developments have resulted from the search for ways of reducing the drain on national gold reserves, the desire to increase sales of American manufactured products abroad, the need to find markets for huge surpluses of farm and dairy produce, and the effort to reduce the risks of American investment abroad. These innovations, essentially domestic in origin, have led to new economic rationales for aid operations, to the development of new forms of aid, and to tightening standards of fiscal management.

Efforts to reduce the gold outflow consisted primarily of "tied dollar" restrictions requiring that aid money be spent in the United States, so that only goods, not gold (or dollars), would change hands. As a result, foreign purchases financed by United States aid fell from over one-half the total aid budget in 1959 to only one-fifth in 1963. By 1964, the total outflow attributed to foreign aid was only half a billion dollars, compared to $2.5 billion spent overseas by tourists and $3 billion in foreign spending by American businessmen that year. Goods used in aid projects overseas now had to be purchased in the United States, regardless of the added cost: in 1960, when aid procurement was subject to worldwide bidding, only 11 per cent of the iron and steel, 11 per cent of the nonferrous metals, and 17 per cent of the fertilizer bought through foreign aid appropriations were purchased in the United States; for 1963, the figures were 87 per cent, 92 per cent, and 97 per cent, respectively. In fact, the aid program was beginning to be among the best customers of certain businesses. In the calendar year 1962, for example, one-third of the exports of U.S.-made locomotives, one-third of the fertilizers, and 21 per cent of the iron and steel products exported from the United States were purchased for foreign aid programs. Sometimes, American products were accepted abroad reluctantly at first; but the AID administrator reported in 1964 that after sampling American goods, some satisfied customers (the Indian Railways, for example) were displaying a "marked preference for American equipment" (in this case, over that supplied by British competitors). He added that "United States foreign aid has probably opened a significant future market for American products."[1]

As early as 1954, laws had authorized the use of surplus food for relief and aid abroad; but for the first few years, the program was little more than a series of pilot projects. Continued government purchases of farm surpluses and congressional pressure to find uses for them

---

[1] Address by Honorable David E. Bell, Mar. 19, 1964 (AID Release 64-60). In the same speech to Dallas businessmen, he mentioned that in recent months "Texas stood first among the states in the volume of AID-financed procurement."

forced the administration to develop new programs, and by the early 1960's, between one-fourth and one-half of all United States economic aid took the form of surplus agricultural commodities. "Food for Peace" became an important part of the Alliance for Progress in Latin America; and by 1965, over 10 million school children—about one-third of the total—received a daily school lunch made up of American agricultural commodities. This project not only improved the diet of these children, it was explained, but also reduced school drop-out rates and thus indirectly contributed to the development of human resources. In many countries elsewhere, proceeds from the sale of United States wheat were used to pay workers for building dams, power plants, and roads. By the mid-1960's, surplus agricultural commodity shipments amounted to well over a billion dollars a year at the somewhat inflated world prices. Experimentation had shown that food surpluses could be used for a variety of purposes, including relief, supplemental aid for workers engaged in development projects, and public sales whose proceeds in local currency were used in support of development projects. But there is evidence that in most countries United States surplus food is less useful than dollar aid would be as a stimulus to development; and as European agricultural producers are also beginning to propose substituting food for monetary aid, there is danger of a general weakening of Western aid as the new investment of hard currencies falls off.[2]

The aid program also began to concentrate on ways to encourage and safeguard American investments in the less developed countries. Left to their own devices, U.S. investments abroad tend to concentrate in European and other industrialized states, where the demand for capital has been great enough to produce generous, and safe, returns. In the less developed countries, however, American capital has ventured only rarely, and then usually in extractive industries like petroleum, mining, and rubber, which many governments now prefer to see under native ownership. In 1962, AID began sharing the costs of investment surveys that might diversify industrial development. AID also began shortly thereafter to catalog commercial opportunities in the less-developed countries, for the benefit of potential investors. Still another incentive to foreign investment was the new AID-sponsored insurance against "political risks" (expropriation, inconvertibility of currency, and war or insurrectionary damage), which became available to protect $1.4 billion in American investments in 58 countries by fiscal year 1964. Even the surplus agricultural commodities program is now used to aid American investors, because a portion of the proceeds is set aside in each country for loans to United States firms doing business there.

[2] Lawrence Witt and Carl Eicher, *The Effects of U.S. Agricultural Surplus Disposal Programs in Recipient Countries* (East Lansing, Mich.: State University Dept. of Agricultural Economics, 1964), p. 9.

The effort to encourage greater American investment in under-developed countries was accompanied by an intensification of United States aid to indigenous private enterprise. National development banks for encouraging and assisting local industry represented one device for this purpose; and in 1964, $125 million was lent to development banks, housing banks, and cooperatives, and another $60 million went directly to local private enterprise. All told, the United States provided technical assistance and "seed loans" to 36 industrial banks in 30 countries. United States missions also encouraged host governments to adopt tax and fiscal policies favorable to private capital.

Other recent developments in the practice of foreign aid also reflected the desire to please influential sectors of the American public. For a variety of reasons, the Kennedy and Johnson administrations decided to decentralize many technical assistance projects. Earlier, contracts had been offered primarily to universities and foundations, in addition to the engineering and construction firms needed for large-scale capital projects. This practice had appeared to develop understanding and support for foreign aid in influential circles throughout the country, and on one or two occasions it was even invoked as a demonstration to congressmen of how the aid program benefited nearly every district. And the use of contracts permitted the recruiting of specialists who might not otherwise be available to the government. Contracts began to involve distinguished institutions as well as individuals in aid operations, thus enlarging the resources available for solving problems in the field. By the 1960's, AID contracts were making use of a wide variety of industries, as well as large farms, labor unions, banks, cooperatives, savings and loan associations, professional groups, universities, and even state and local governments.

The fact that American aid has responded so massively to its own domestic politics should not be regarded as necessarily base or irrelevant to its purposes. American foreign policy must remain an expression of its source. Apart from the dangers to the survival of any economic program that indefinitely tried to thwart or ignore the self-interest of American economy, the probabilities are that the pace of economic development overseas has been accelerated by the encouragement of local private initiative, for example, as well as by the injection of foreign private capital. Usually the countries that have enjoyed the most rapid growth rates have made use of private capital, even though for a variety of political reasons the host governments themselves may have not desired to encourage such initiative from private sources. And the U.S. was flexible enough to offer most of its aid to India through the public sector.

Nor should it be assumed that the only factors that influenced the development of United States foreign aid programs over the years were

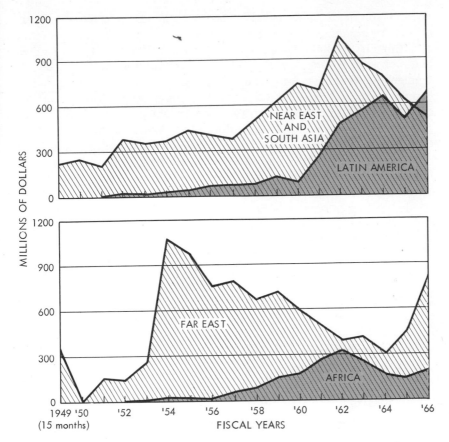

Trend of economic assistance from AID and predecessor agencies

internal politics. The broad outlines of the program, especially its dimensions and its areas of concentration, are also responsive to world conditions (as seen in Washington, to be sure). Marshall Plan aid to Europe was America's response to what it perceived as the greatest crisis of the postwar years. The Korean War, in which American initiative produced a defense against Communist aggression in the underdeveloped world, led to an aid focused on the periphery of China and the Soviet Union. In the early 1960's, the United States was beginning to respond to a shocked discovery that all was not well in Latin America; whereas from 1948 to 1960, the United States had given only about 2 per cent of its economic aid to Latin America, by 1965 about one-fourth of it was going to that area, which was receiving more assistance per person than any other region.

In addition to the shifts in regional emphasis and international purposes of American aid, changes in the program also followed developments in the factual knowledge and basic theory underlying its operations. An earlier chapter describes the phases in which the program relied at first exclusively on capital, then added technical assistance, and more recently, approaches to institution-building and social development. Another conceptual change has been the trend from scattered country programs, consisting of a series of unrelated projects, to a more comprehensive integrated country development plan.

While American aid is still offered to provide a national presence in a variety of situations, increasingly, an effort is made to concentrate aid resources in countries and projects over a sustained period of time, in order to achieve a real impact. Thus the 1965 program concentrated 67 per cent of its development loans in seven countries; 78 per cent of its "supporting assistance" in four countries; and 64 per cent of its military assistance in eleven countries. Nearly 90 per cent of all AID assistance was destined for twenty-five countries. And finally, the long time dimensions of aid were gaining recognition in spite of pressures against program continuity, such as rotation of both technicians and administrators, sensitivity to criticism from projects as they reached the inevitable plateaus of development, and the glittering appeal of something different. Most professionals in Washington now believe that periods of ten years or longer might be required in large-scale institution-building or mass diffusion projects.

The need to recapture and analyze the experiences of the past decade led to the first efforts to use research in order to improve operational effectiveness. In 1959–1960, a special Technical Assistance Study Group examined the experiences of nearly 1,000 technicians returning from assignments in all parts of the world. Like much foreign aid research, the project was never completed, but much useful information nevertheless became available for study and training. Even more elaborate research projects were undertaken under the Foreign Assistance Act of 1961, which authorized an annual research budget that grew to more than $10 million by the mid-1960's.

In some cases, these trends have improved the use of American resources for encouraging and influencing the speed and direction of development. Some administration responses to domestic pressures, it is true, have resulted in restrictions on project choices and operational flexibility, including legislative discriminations against certain nations. But others have led to innovations in programs and operations—such as the Food for Peace Program, the Peace Corps, decentralization of technical assistance to private contractors, and encouragement of private enterprise.

Recent trends in the American aid operations have recognized the possibility of using new resources and approaches. They have permitted increasing use of foreign aid as a lever to reform. They have elongated

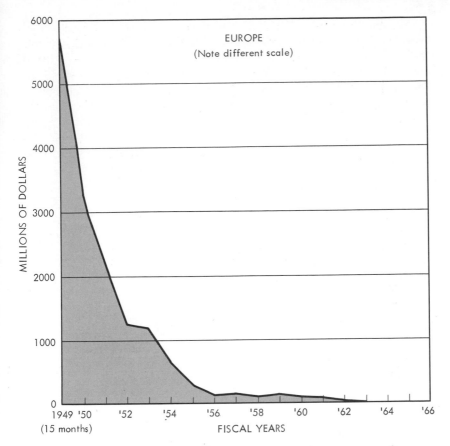

EUROPE
(Note different scale)

Trend of economic assistance from AID and predecessor agencies

its shadow by supporting institutions devoted to change. And they have enlarged the economic perspective of aid by applying the test of self-sustaining growth to programming. They have thus reflected increasingly the pluralism and the diversity of the American society. But they have also represented the growing recognition that the United States cannot bear the burden alone. The programs of other countries and international agencies have become increasingly important in United States foreign policy.

EUROPEAN AND INTERNATIONAL AID PROGRAMS

During the past decade, more than a score of nations from both sides of the Iron Curtain have been offering foreign aid. Through the Organization for Economic Cooperation and Development (OECD), Austria, Belgium, Canada, Denmark, France, Germany, Italy, Japan,

Netherlands, Norway, Portugal, Sweeden, the United Kingdom, and the U.S. coordinate their aid offerings, and still other countries, including Australia, Kuwait, New Zealand, Switzerland, and Israel offer aid independently in a variety of forms. Between 1956 and 1964 the European nations had offered about the same amount of aid to the underdeveloped world that United States had invested in European recovery under the Marshall Plan in 1948 to 1952—something over $13 billion. Although European aid funds were at first channeled to former colonies, more and more was now being offered without such restrictions. Thus although about two-thirds of all external aid to Africa came from West Europe, France was also assisting Mexico and Greece; Britain was offering technical assistance in Latin America; and France, The Netherlands, and Italy were contributing heavily to the World Bank consortium aiding India and Pakistan. Germany, Canada, and Japan, with no recent colonial tradition, also had substantial aid programs of their own. In 1962, 44 per cent of the noncommunist aid was provided through sources other than United States bilateral programs. By 1965, the figure was more than half.

The European donors have also begun to feel the effects of new foreign aid programs in their domestic politics. Once, few citizens had objected to programs offered out of respect for "former ties" to colonies (France and Britain), or where they substituted for reparations (Germany, Japan, and Italy), or to carry out what was perceived as national obligations (Israel, Scandinavia, and The Netherlands).[3] But in the decade of the 1960's, foreign aid had begun to take on a rationale of its own, independent from these traditions; and in the process, it received more domestic attention. In Britain, both political parties had supported Commonwealth aid; and soon after the election of 1964, the Labor government established a Ministry of Overseas Development, bringing together appropriate staff from the Colonial Office, the Commonwealth Relations Office, and the Foreign Office. In France, Raymond Cartier led a vocal opposition to foreign aid in the face of domestic need, but the Jeanneney Report countered with a new, compelling view of the responsibilities of national leadership as a spur to foreign aid. In Germany, opposition from the powerful states of the Federal Republic, combined with the indifference of the business community and the public, forced the federal government to proceed slowly.

Individual efforts of European nations were greatly strengthened when the Development Assistance Committee of OECD moved to coordinate the bilateral activities of member nations. By working together in confidential sessions, the national representatives were able to de-

---

[3] Robert E. Asher "How to Succeed in Foreign Aid Without Really Trying," in *Public Policy*, ed. John D. Montgomery and Arthur Smithies (Cambridge: Harvard University, distributors, 1964), XIII, 109-32.

velop an increasingly professional attitude toward their common problems. Through the technique of "confrontation diplomacy," first developed in administering the Marshall Plan, OECD nations now began to apply gentle pressure on members that were not living up to the standards of the group. Results were not long in coming: Canada, embarrassed at finding its aid level at the bottom of the list, increased its effort, and the United Kingdom, which had preferred to use commercial rates for its development loans, began to make them more suitable to development needs by moving toward interest-free loans.[4]

By the mid-1960's, the trend toward international cooperation in foreign aid had permitted more flexibility in World Bank operations as well. Over 100 member states had contributed to the World Bank (IBRD, or International Bank for Reconstruction and Development), enabling it to lend $8 billion in "hard" loans at something approaching commercial rates. But the IBRD slowly began to recognize the need for noncommercial credit to support development projects that were necessary but not directly income producing; and in January 1960, it created the "soft-loan" International Development Association. The terms of its first $1 billion in loans offered 10 years of grace before any repayments were due, followed by another 10-year period during which the principal was repaid at only 1 per cent per year. In some cases, these loans were so soft that the principal did not become a major part of the payment for 30 years. By blending hard and soft loans, IBRD and IDA were able to accommodate the capital needs of almost any variety.

The World Bank had begun conservatively, preferring to use its funds to support the growth of private capitalism. It continued to exert itself on behalf of free enterprise, announcing during 1964 its intention to provide loans to the International Finance Corporation (IFC) for relending to private industry. But IBRD imparted no doctrinal flavor to these activities, since some of its own member nations preferred mixed or statist economies. In its preference for businesslike procedures, the bank began to work toward a code of international financial behavior that applied to any form of economic organization. The principal features of this unwritten code began to appear from its operations as it denied loans to some countries in preference to others. Indonesia received no aid, for example, because of its history of expropriating private property without compensation; and Greece was denied because of its defaults on international debts. In the case of Spain, IBRD loans were withheld pending changes in its fiscal policies, especially those involving political control over economic development and the use of patronage in its industrialization effort. And when the recom-

---

[4] Milton J. Esman, "Europe in the Common Aid Effort," in *Public Policy*, ed. John D. Montgomery and Arthur Smithies (Cambridge: Harvard University, distributors, 1965), Vol. XIV.

mended changes were made, entrepreneurial activities increased, the bank prepared a survey of Spanish economic needs, and the ban was lifted: Spain received the credit it needed for its industrial development. The bank has gradually extended credit to countries experimenting with other economic systems as well. If the Fascist state of Spain received bank aid, so did a Communist one, Yugoslavia.

The World Bank also offers other forms of aid. It trains economic planners through its Economic Development Institute, and its good offices are available to relieve international tensions that impede development. It was the World Bank that mediated the issue of compensation for the Suez Canal after Nasser had seized it; and at the request of both parties, the World Bank provided advisers to represent the Congo and Belgium after the former's independence. Bank initiatives also provided for the consortium of nations aiding Pakistan and India in the development of the Indus River Basin. The example of the World Bank was followed by the Alliance for Progress. The Inter-American Development Bank administers not only the conventional development loans from its own funds, but also the United States-financed Social Progress Trust Fund. These activities lent a total of $162 million in fiscal year 1964.

The World Bank is only one of the specialized agencies of the United Nations engaged in economic development activities. In its first six years, the UN Special Fund, a "pump-primer" created to stimulate the flow of deevlopment capital, spent $16 million to conduct pre-investment surveys that brought forth investments of $780 million from other sources. By 1965, over 400 of its pre-investment projects had been approved. The United Nations Special Fund activities, led by a distinguished American industrialist and foreign aid administrator, continued to display partiality toward private investment, however, and it received severe criticism from the Soviet Union for using its funds to encourage private investment rather than to enter into the operations itself. The Soviet Union also complained because Western nations, notably England and the United States, had received the largest contracts for conducting investment surveys.[5] Even international aid programs were not free from politics.

The UN also offers advisory assistance in a variety of technical fields. Since the early 1950's it has appointed individual experts upon request of member governments. By the mid-1960's, efforts were under way to reorganize the Special Fund and the technical assistance of the UN to permit comprehensive country programming.[6] In the meantime,

---

[5] *The New York Times,* Jan. 13, 1965.

[6] The trend to apply American country programming techniques to UN operations was sharply criticized by Karl Mathiasen in a report to be published by The Brookings Institution.

the World Health Organization, International Labor Organization, Civil Aviation Board, Food and Agricultural Organization, and other specialized agencies continued to conduct projects in their specialized fields, many of which directly benefited the underdeveloped countries.

In spite of the increase of international development activities, there has been, if anything, less competitiveness among the Western donors than in the earlier years of the postcolonial period. Each donor began to seek ways of capitalizing on its own resources and approaches without detracting from the efforts of others. Far from feeling competitive, Americans allowed their efforts to decline relatively during the early years of the 1960's, as contributions of other nations and by international bodies (with heavy American participation) rose.

Because the need for capital and other forms of aid was rising still faster, however, there was ample room for aid programs sponsored by the Soviet Union and China.

THE COMMUNIST AID PROGRAMS

Once the USSR had embarked upon its own foreign aid program soon after 1950, the age of Stalin's autarchic isolationism was over, and some favorite Communist theories ended with it. Soviet expectations had already been disappointed over the continued vitality of the capitalist system after World War II. Moreover, the rise of independent nationalism in the colonies proved to be much harder for the Soviet Union to exploit than the proletariat-led social revolutions it had hoped for. The American responses to these conditions must have been instructive to Stalin's successors: the resurgence of Europe under the Marshall Plan and the first fruits of Truman's "bold new program" of Point 4 in the underdeveloped countries were marks of a successful initiative that the Kremlin leaders decided it was necessary to counter. Like the atom bomb, foreign aid soon lost the character of an American monopoly.

The Soviet Union, like the United States, did not at once discover the wide variety of diplomatic purposes that foreign aid could serve. At first, the USSR offered spectacular "presence" or impact projects without reference to their economic usefulness or practicality, and it used sudden demonstrations of Soviet friendship to encourage neutralism and to prevent the development of close ties with the West. The USSR built showplace polytechnic institutes and luxurious hotels in Guinea and Burma, conspicuous sport stadiums in Indonesia and Guinea, and impressive hospitals in Indonesia and Cambodia. As time passed, however, the USSR found ways of offering "spectaculars" that were not luxuries. The Soviets built steel plants at Bhilai, India, that proved to be more economical and efficient than either British or German plants in that country; they agreed to build the Aswan Dam after the United States and the World Bank had withdrawn from the project; and in spite of the great technical difficulties, they proceeded on schedule.

The Soviet achievements in foreign aid were accompanied by failures that would be recognized by any well-read American congressman. Like American efforts, Communist aid projects did not bring magical political results. Guinea, a heavy beneficiary, did not hesitate to expel the Soviet ambassador for interfering with domestic affairs, or to deny the Soviets the use of an airport they had built in Conakry, even in the emergency of the Cuban missile crisis. Burma turned the management of their Soviet-built hotel over to an Israeli firm, and later reduced its patronage by refusing to allow tourists to remain in the country more than 24 hours. Indonesia, in debt for $1 billion worth of bloc economic and military aid, decided against Soviet advice to withdraw from the UN. Guinea, Egypt, and Indonesia were unable to keep up payments on their aid loans. Egypt, Algeria, and Iraq began to arrest and even execute local Communists. And private citizens in the Soviet Union and East Europe began to resent the fact that goods needed at home were being shipped to ungrateful neutral nations.

Perhaps the most discouraging of all to the Kremlin was the aftermath of the $1 billion aid loan to China, when Peking began competing with the USSR for influence in India, North Vietnam, and Africa and among Communist parties throughout the world. Chinese propaganda was especially annoying to the Soviets because Peking began citing its own experience with Soviet aid to testify that the USSR invaded the sovereignty of other nations, interfered in their domestic affairs, did not really understand the less developed countries, and in fact was little better than the white imperialist nations of Europe and America. The Chinese strategic interest in most of these areas was uncompromisingly revolutionary, while those of the Soviet Union favored a more moderate course sufficiently stabilizing to permit them to concentrate on their own domestic problems without arousing the West.

Chinese aid to Africa has been small: just large enough to make immediate political gains (as often at the expense of the Soviet Union as of the Western powers). Thus Soviet credit to Algeria was $100 million to China's $50 million; in Ghana, the score was $81 million to $20 million; in Mali $55 million to $20 million; and in Guinea $80 million to $24 million.[7] But the Chinese effort had the net effect of keeping the Soviets involved, perhaps on a larger scale than it would choose, and certainly for more difficult long-term purposes than the Chinese have chosen to serve. By the end of the 1950's, the USSR had already

---

[7] Robert A. Scalapino, "Sino-Soviet Competition in Africa," *Foreign Affairs,* XLII, No. 4 (July, 1964), p. 649.

begun to lose its claim to revolutionary leadership in many parts of the world, largely because of Chinese competition. The Chinese, for their part, were able to increase the number of African states recognizing their government from 0 to 14 by mid-1964, and their aid enabled rebel leaders in the Congo and elsewhere to keep both the USSR and the Western powers off balance.

· If the political responses to their aid were less than completely satisfactory, it also became evident that technical difficulties were increasing for the Soviets. Once the easy impact projects had lost their appeal, the really difficult problems of economic development appeared. Soviet technicians began to encounter the same problems that had been confronting Americans working in the tropical environments where their techniques did not readily apply. Like Americans, Soviet technicians began running into cultural, social, and psychological resistance to innovation, finding administrative obstacles that they had not anticipated, and encountering difficulties in getting the host governments to adopt policies necessary for the success of their projects. Moreover, the Communists faced additional difficulties that were peculiar to their system. On high priority projects, they could move faster than the West; but for the rest, the centralized decision-making bureaucracy of the Soviet Union proved to be even slower than that of the United States; and the USSR had no private contractors on which it could call to supplement the planning and managerial resources of the government. The Soviets could train and assign their technicians pretty much at will, without having to compete for them as Americans did. They could even forbid them the use of alcohol and make it stick, as they did in an Indian project. But few of them spoke French or English, which are used as second languages in most of the underdeveloped countries; and because it would have been costly and inefficient to train them in the exotic languages of Africa and Asia, they often had to rely heavily on interpreters working through these secondary languages. Moscow could admit students and other trainees to its universities, regardless of their linguistic and academic qualifications, but found it hard to cope with Africans' resentment at being segregated outside the mainstream of Soviet education, where the standards of instruction were obviously higher. The Soviet Union could accept local products in repayment of loans, but Burma found that the Soviet Union paid prices that were too low; Syria found that the Soviet market was unsteady; and Ghana, Greece, and Egypt found that their products were being dumped on world markets. And to top it all, Soviet goods, especially consumer items, seldom compared favorably in quality with those of the West. Deliveries were slow, and spare parts were hard to get because there were so few established commercial channels upon which buyers and sellers could rely for support.

As projects slowly got underway, the size of the Sino-Soviet aid effort gradually increased, starting with about $100 million per year in the 1950's and rising between $450 million and $500 million in 1965. The total cumulative aid expenditure by the end of 1965 was about $2.6 billion. In their promises, the Communist countries showed an even sharper rise: from $325 million committed in 1962, and $360 million in 1963, to $1.7 billion in 1964 and $1.2 billion in 1965, after the Sino-Soviet split could no longer be concealed. The total commitments by the Communist bloc from the beginning were $7.7 billion —or which, as already indicated, only a little over one-third had actually been spent. Military aid from the Communist bloc, from 1955 to 1964, amounted to over $3 billion, most of which had been delivered by the end of that period.

About half of the new Communist aid was going to the United Arab Republic and India. China concentrated its aid on Africa and Pakistan, where light industries were being built in the expectation of a quick impact on the consumer markets. The Soviet Union, like Western donors, was increasingly concentrating on economically productive projects (like steel mills) that could be financed customarily in 12 years at 2½ per cent interest (in the West, the interest had ranged from some U.S. loans at .7 per cent to 3½ per cent to rates of 5¾ per cent for the Export-Import Bank and World Bank; on the other hand, longer terms of payment were available from all these Western sources). Aside from the effort in Cuba, 10,000 or more Communist technicians were working in over 30 countries, mostly from the USSR. Their numbers were more than double those sent by the United States to twice as many countries.

Just as the United States and Europe were improving the degree of coordination among themselves, permitting the United States to level off its effort, conflict in the former Sino-Soviet bloc was increasing, forcing a faster pace of spending. For a time the long-range approach to economic development, which the Soviet Union was beginning to show, seemed difficult to sustain as the Chinese began to seize the initiative and enjoy the short-lived applause that impact projects brought. But for a change, the Western world enjoyed the luxury of watching others commit errors in the haste of competitive giving. Only when the Chinese economy began to display its weakness abroad did the Soviet position as chief Communist aid-giver permit the return of economic rationality.

The fact remained, however, that so long as one nation could use even a relatively small aid program to support the prestige of local revolutionaries, the world was still not a very safe place.

THE PROBLEMS AHEAD

The laurels bestowed a decade ago upon the United States for excellence in foreign aid might have withered somewhat by the 1960's, but there was already evidence that the United States was beginning to rest on them. After 1955, the aid budget had begun to take a smaller and smaller proportion of America's wealth, not because there was great satisfaction with results, but because there was indifference, disillusionment, and even despair. The 1949 aid appropriation was 11.5 per cent of the federal budget, but the 1966 appropriation was less than 3 per cent. In spite of the growing gap between the per capita incomes of rich and poor nations, there was still no conviction among the makers of American foreign policy that greater United States efforts were needed.

Yet the need for external assistance was continuing to increase so rapidly that there was reasonable doubt whether the economies of the Western donors—to say nothing of their politics—could supply it. Various economists predicted that by 1970 the foreign exchange gap of the less developed countries might be between $12 billion and $20 billion per year. In spite of their visible progress, nearly one-half of the human race was living on an average yearly income below $100. A very large proportion of this population—about 25 per cent—was between the ages of one and five, and 70 per cent suffered from malnutrition so serious that half of them died before reaching the age of five. The AID director pointed out in 1964 that unless the aid level from the West was doubled by 1970, the slow growth of per capita income that these nations had achieved would level off, with political consequences that were incalculable. In the meantime, however, the relative volume of United States dollar aid was actually declining.

In the hope of achieving real progress in at least a few areas, American aid concentrated on those where the prospects seemed best. In India and Pakistan, where large United States programs were at work, a per capita growth rate of 3 per cent per year was considered possible (although it represented a higher rate than the United States economy achieved over the past 50 years). Over a period of 25 years, this rate would double the per capita income to $150 yearly—not a handsome figure compared with the projected United States increase over the same period from $2,500 to $4,000, but enough to educate all primary school children (instead of half, as at present) and virtually to eliminate diseases such as malaria, typhoid, smallpox, and cholera. Such improvements would permit these nations to make better use of their human resources, generate more savings and investment, increase incentives, and introduce technological advances that would generate further development.

The increasing economic sophistication of American and international aid efforts has led to experimentation with new techniques of country programming, concentration of effort, and self-help standards. If these approaches were to become accepted international practice, the economic potential of even present aid levels could increase measurably.

There is also evidence, in spite of the growing gap between rich and poor nations in terms of per capita income, that in other respects the underdeveloped areas are improving their relative position. Their education and public health standards, starting from a lower base, are improving faster than those of the industrialized nations in many cases; some poor countries invest greater proportions of their resources in growth-producing programs than affluent countries do, especially in industrialization; and some of the "middle" countries are growing faster than the richest ones.[8] The fact remains, however, that in the 1960's, the increases in economic effort did not approach the minimum predicted requirements for the decade ahead. It was possible to draw satisfaction from the many economic achievements that foreign aid had already introduced, without feeling confidence that future needs were being faced realistically. The greatest unresolved problem ahead for United States foreign aid was developing the rational political consensus needed for the future. The uncertainty of executive, legislative, and public support was evident throughout the United States aid program, from its recruiting offices to the hesitant and indecisive posture of its mission abroad.

The greatest operating problem of the 1950's—administrative continuity—was still not resolved in the 1960's. There were still congressmen who considered aid a temporary measure, as had been unwisely suggested a decade before; there was still uncertainty whether it belonged in or out of the State Department; and public apathy still permitted minor and major domestic conveniences to distort foreign operations. In 1962, David Bell became the eleventh director of aid operations in 15 years, during which period the agency had to reorganize itself at least five times (see accompanying chart). The 1961 reorganization looked stable enough at first, but the familiar signs of congressional dissatisfaction were still evident. In 1965 there was still congressional support for phasing out the existing foreign aid program within two years in order to force another reorganization. And there was still confused responsibility in Washington. Although the Agency for International Development now included both the capital and the technical assistance components of large-scale economic programming, the military program was largely outside its administrative juris-

[8] See, for example, Hans W. Singer, "Social Development: Key Growth Sector," *International Development Review,* VII, No. 1 (March, 1965).

Changes in U.S. foreign aid administration and aid programs of other federal departments (excluding Export-Import Bank, Peace Corps, and Food for Peace)

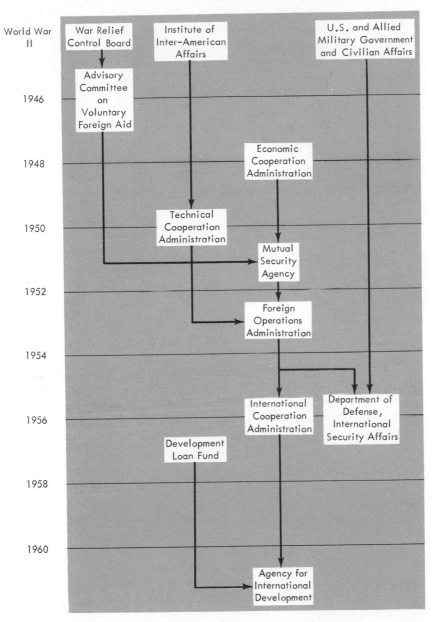

diction, and nearly 30 other executive agencies were still engaged in overseas operations. There had been improvements in the internal organization of AID, to support the country programming concept that had begun to develop during the late 1950's, but timely responses to requests from the field were still difficult to achieve for the 2,200,000 messages that came to AID in Washington every month, most of which required some form of action and response. Beginning in 1963, AID began to reduce its headquarters staff in the hope of streamlining the organization. At the same time, it began as a matter of policy to delegate increasing authority to field missions and to private contractors for carrying out broad lines of policy. If an excess of personnel was responsible for delays in reaching timely decisions, AID had found a prescription for efficiency. But congressional and public response to the decentralization, though sympathetic, still registered dissatisfaction when it came to authorizing and appropriating funds. And the net result would depend, as always, more on the quality than on the quantity of personnel or on administrative improvements. But neither the political climate in which the agency struggled nor the political uncertainty of an AID career made recruiting any easier.

Congressional and public disillusionment with foreign aid continued to grow with the disappointment over political responses in the recipient countries. The economic and technological gains that foreign aid had introduced were no consolation when Sukarno was reported to have told the United States to "go to hell" with its aid, in the same cold winter that Nasser advised the Americans to "jump in the lake," and France, one of the largest recipients of the Marshall Plan aid, took the lead in disassembling American policy in the United Nations, the Atlantic Community, and in Southeast Asia.

The intransigency of the world situation in which the United States was exercising its diplomacy was as frustrating at top levels as it was in the rice paddies of Southeast Asia where American soldiers were trying to restrain the Communist advance. Perhaps the epitaph of the 1960's would be this octave displayed over the bar of the Officers' Club at Banmethuot, Vietnam, during the first frustrations of the Advisors' War:

> It's not my job to run this train
> The whistle I can't blow.
> It's not my job to say how far
> This train's allowed to go.
> It's not my job to blow off steam
> Or even ring the bell,
> But let this train run off the track
> And see who catches hell.

The 1960's were an uncomfortable period for the foreign policies of the West. The generation that had fought the most destructive war in history had also installed and set in motion vast international machinery for negotiation, technological and capital diffusion, and even peace-keeping: but it was finding difficulty in sustaining an effort, the largest result of which seemed to be staving off doomsday. It would still be left to the generation of the Peace Corps and the sit-ins to supply the mixture of imagination and patience required to fulfill the promise of the twentieth century.

The decade of development was notable for its teach-ins and peace pickets, however, as well as for its sit-ins and Peace Corpsmen. Idealists who wanted to demonstrate the force of social morality in domestic politics were among the first to challenge conceptions of world leadership being offered in Washington. The moral tide carried with it a widespread disillusionment over the uses of national power. Military adventures were beginning to produce some turn-of-the-century overtones as many Americans began to wonder whether twenty-five years of war, reconstruction, foreign aid, and containment after 1940 had not already paid in full the national debt of twenty years of isolationism between the two world wars. There was a Broadway show entitled *Stop the World: I Want to Get Off*, and the presidential campaign of a major party candidate seemed to be waged with that slogan.

But the show ended, the campaign was lost, and the world displayed no signs that it would come to a stop—unless by its own destruction. The effort to change that still plausible ending included disarmament talks, test ban treaties, alliances, and summit conferences. But these activities involved only the major powers. It was left to foreign aid to deal with the others.

Among the fifteen to twenty nations that may possess nuclear weapons by 1980, some were receiving foreign aid in 1960. Their leaders were not, of course, grateful for their condition, and no amount of economic assistance would make them so. Strategic foreign aid was not intended to produce gratitude, but to identify them with the forces of modernization. Most statesmen in the underdeveloped countries were convinced that their own position in world history would be measured by the extent to which they had identified themselves and their nations with hopeful change. They were agreed that such an identification could occur either through rebellion and civil war against richer and more powerful nations that repudiated them, or that it could take place with their assistance. Most still preferred the latter course.

The current struggle of humanity against privation and injustice has taken new forms in recent decades. For the first time it became imperative for the rich nations to find common cause with the poor in order to avert their common ruin. The difficulty remained in getting started and keeping the momentum. The United States had made the start because it had the power, the imagination—and the presumption—to do so. But its efforts had been joined by those of others until, by the 1960's, the American burden was equally shared by its principal European allies.

The risks of failure rose with the divisiveness of the Congo, Vietnam, and the Dominican Republic. Each setback in a national development program in Latin America or Asia was a reminder that change was occurring, whether according to plan or not. There was not always the choice of using the gentle means of economic aid in bringing about hopeful developments. But where the choice existed, the mood appropriate to the hour was not that invoked at the beginning of this book by Henry Adams' words, but that of another famous American:

> As life is action and passion, it is required of a man that he should share the passion and action of his time at the price of being judged not to have lived.[9]

The question of the 1960's was not whether military power could contain the spread of communism, but whether economic power could create conditions that would make communism unnecessary.

[9] Oliver Wendell Holmes, Jr., Memorial Day Address, 1884.

Bibliography

Alba, Victor, *Alliance Without Allies: Mythology of Progress in Latin America.* New York: Praeger, 1965. Polemical attack on Latin American social structure and on the modesty of the reform contemplated by the Alliance for Progress.

Alhaique, C., *Italian Industry and International Technical Cooperation.* New York: Heinman, 1965.

Amuzegar, Jahangir, *Theory and Practice of Technical Assistance.* New York: Praeger, 1965.

Arensberg, Conrad M., and Arthur H. Niehoff, *Introducing Social Change.* Chicago: Aldine, 1964. A manual designed to prepare U. S. technicians for overseas development assignments, using valuable insights from anthropology and sociology to explain the processes of acculturation.

Arnold, H. J. P., *Aid for Developing Countries, A Comparative Study.* Chester Springs, Pa.: Dufour Editions, 1962. Good general survey of U. S., British, West European, Soviet, and multilateral aid as of 1959.

Asher, Robert E., *Grants, Loans, and Local Currencies: Their Role in Foreign Aid.* Washington, D. C.: Brookings Institution, 1961. A clearly reasoned analysis of the respective advantages of grants and loans and their impact on the economies of the beneficiary nations.

————, *et al., Development of the Emerging Countries, An Agenda For Research.* Washington, D. C.: Brookings Institution, 1962. Thoughtful and provocative essays on research needs for the Decade of Development.

Avramović, Dragoslav, *Debt Servicing Capacity and Postwar Growth in International Public Indebtedness.* Baltimore: Johns Hopkins, 1960. Careful, guarded analysis of growth rates, investment flows, and national debts, offering generally optimistic view of the possibility of economic advance through wise use of credit resources under the leadership of the World Bank.

————, *et al., Economic Growth and External Debt.* Baltimore: Johns Hopkins, 1964.

Badeau, John S. and Georgiana G. Stevens, *Bread from Stones, Fifty Years of Technical Assistance.* Englewood Cliffs, N. J.: Prentice-Hall, 1966.

Barish, N. N. and M. Verhulst, eds., *Management Sciences in the Emerging Countries.* New York: Macmillan, 1965.

Basch, Antonin, *Financing Economic Development.* New York: Macmillan, 1964.

Bauer, P. T., *United States Aid and Indian Economic Development.* Washington, D. C.: American Enterprise Assoc., 1959. An interesting and well-argued proposal to use U.S. aid to India as a means of influencing economic policy in that nation in the direction of private enterprise.

Benham, Frederic, *Economic Aid to Underdeveloped Countries.* London: Oxford University Press, 1961. Good, short, sensible statement of economic requirements (specifically of grant aid) for development purposes.

Berliner, Joseph S., *Soviet Economic Aid: The New Aid and Trade Policy in Underdeveloped Countries.* New York: Praeger, 1958. Standard work on the subject. Most of its conclusions are still relevant and valid.

NOTE: Items deal primarily with foreign aid, plus selected books dealing with the economics of development. In some cases, volumes are listed without comment because they were not available at the time this bibliography was prepared. Articles and government documents have not been included. Students who wish to consult official documents concerned with foreign aid should examine reports of the Senate Committee on Foreign Relations and Committee on Appropriations, and the House Committee on Foreign Affairs and Committee on Appropriations (especially its Subcommittee on Governmental Operations). In addition, special study reports dealing with foreign aid are published from time to time by these sources. The Agency for International Development, the International Development Bank for Reconstruction and Development, the United Nations, and the specialized agencies of the United Nations publish reports and documents relating to foreign aid.

Bigelow, K. W., *Problems and Prospects of Education in Africa*. Cambridge: Harvard University, 1965.

Billerbeck, Klaus, *Soviet Bloc Foreign Aid to the Underdeveloped Countries: An Analysis and Prognosis*. Hamburg: Archives of World Economy, 1960. Careful, systematic examination of Soviet and Western approaches to foreign aid, relatively free from ideological bias.

Bingham, Jonathan B., *Shirt-Sleeve Diplomacy: Point 4 in Action*. New York: John Day, 1953. Series of vignettes, reminiscences, and reflections about the life of a foreign aid administrator, entertainingly told.

Black, Eugene R., *The Diplomacy of Economic Development*. Cambridge: Harvard University, 1960. Good, short, popular introduction to capital assistance operations, by the distinguished former president of the World Bank.

Blelloch, David H., *Aid for Development*. London: Fabian International Bureau, 1958.

Bock, Edwin A., *Fifty Years of Technical Assistance*. Chicago: Public Administration Clearing House, 1954. Useful lessons suggested by 55 interviewees with a variety of technical assistance experience abroad.

Brown, William A. and Redvers Opie, *American Foreign Assistance*. Washington, D. C.: Brookings Institution, 1953. Indispensable history of the early foreign aid efforts.

Byrnes, Francis C., *Americans in Technical Assistance, A Study of Attitudes and Responses to Their Role Abroad*. New York: Praeger, 1965. Analytical report of surveys and interviews with former employees of International Cooperation Administration, presenting data on the nature of technical assistance as well as individual attitudes among many practitioners.

Calder, Ritchie, *Two-way Passage, A Study of the Give-and-Take of International Aid*. London: Heinemann, 1964. Humanistic view of aid as a contribution to a world culture.

Castle, Eugene W., *Billions, Blunders, and Baloney: The Fantastic Story of How Uncle Sam Is Squandering Your Money Overseas*. New York: Devin-Adair, 1955. Unreliable diatribe against the "wasteful" practices of U. S. overseas development programs.

Cerych, Ladislav, *Problems of Aid to Education in Developing Countries*. New York: Praeger, 1965. Careful review of the major educational planning efforts in the LDC's and of the actual and possible role of foreign aid in supporting them.

Chandrasekhar, S., *American Aid and India's Economic Development*. New York: Praeger, 1966. Sympathetic description of American aid projects in India, displaying more attention to Indian than to American weaknesses in theory and practice.

Cleveland, Harlan, C. J. Mangone, and J. C. Adams, *The Overseas Americans*. New York: McGraw-Hill, 1960. A pioneering study of the demands of a technical assistance assignment and life overseas, powered by Cleveland's intuitions and tempered by his sparkling wit, but marred by serious methodological deficiencies.

Coffin, Frank, *Witness for Aid*. Boston: Houghton-Mifflin, 1964. Passionate, sometimes eloquent defense of U. S. aid operations, with recommendations for more serious national commitment.

Coombs, P. H., *Education and Foreign Aid: Ways to Improve United States Foreign Educational Aid*. Cambridge: Harvard University, 1965.

Curle, A., *Educational Strategy for Developing Societies, A Study of Educational and Social Factors in Relation to Economic Growth*. London: Tavistock, 1963. Reflections on the condition of underdevelopment, with good advice on strategies and priorities.

Curti, Merle and Kendall Birr, *Prelude to Point Four: American Technical Missions Overseas 1838–1938*. Madison: University of Wisconsin, 1954. Useful case histories of informal American technical assistance activities abroad, with sober conclusions for any who expect easy success and long-term impact from small advisory projects.

Dreier, J., ed., *The Alliance for Progress: Problems and Prospects*. Baltimore: Johns Hopkins, 1962.

Elliott, William Y., *Education and Training in the Developing Countries, The Role of U. S. Foreign Aid*. New York: Praeger, 1966. A searching inquiry into the requirements and implications of the educational component in national development and foreign aid, based on papers developed at Harvard University seminars.

——, Chairman of study group, *The Political Economy of American Foreign Policy, Its Concepts, Strategy, and Limits*. New York: Holt, 1955. A remarkably prescient and still useful examination of the relationships between the national economy and U.S. foreign policy.

Erasmus, C. J., *Man Takes Control: Cultural Development and American Aid*. Minneapolis: University of Minnesota, 1961. Studies of technical improvement through foreign aid projects, focusing on motivations to change, covering both individual and social elements, and offering valuable insights into the relevance of social science research for foreign aid operations.

Fatouros, A. A. and Robert N. Kelson, *Canada's Overseas Aid*. Canadian Institute of International Affairs, 1964.

Feis, Herbert, *Diplomacy of the Dollar*. Baltimore: Johns Hopkins, 1950. Interesting account of interregnum efforts to use private foreign investments as an instrument of foreign policy.

——, *Foreign Aid and Foreign Policy*. New York: St. Martin's Press, 1964. A polished, idiosyncratic statement by a distinguished historian of theories of "material improvement" and of the coming of foreign aid for diplomatic purposes. Contains trenchant comments on bilateral and multilateral approaches and policy dilemmas.

Foster, George M., *Traditional Cultures and the Impact of Technological Change*. New York: Harper, 1962. Very good summary of anthropological knowledge about the nature, processes, and inducing of culture change, especially in peasant societies, couched in terms useful to technical assistants.

Gardner, John W., *AID and the Universities: A Report of the Administrator of The Agency for International Development*. Washington, D. C.: Agency for International Development, 1964. The influential "Gardner Report" recommending improvements in AID's use of, and relations with, universities.

Gardner, Richard W., *New Directions in U. S. Foreign Economic Policy*. New York: Foreign Policy Association, Headline Series No. 133, 1959. Introductory description of aid and trade in U. S. diplomacy, with sensible but by now obvious recommendations.

Gideonse, H. D., *Economic Foreign Policy of the United States*. Cairo: National Bank of Egypt, 1953. Three short but penetrating lectures describing the American concern with world politics that led to the first foreign aid programs; designed for foreign ears but still relevant to Americans.

Glick, Philip M., *The Administration of Technical Assistance: Growth in the Americas*. Chicago: University of Chicago, 1957. Useful analysis of the administration of U.S. aid to Latin America, with comparative reference to different U.S. and UN approaches.

Goldwin, Robert A., *Why Foreign Aid?* Chicago: Rand McNally, 1962. Probably the best short collection of reprinted and new essays on foreign aid.

Goodenough, Ward Hunt, *Cooperation in Change, an Anthropological Approach to Community Development*. New York: Russell Sage Foundation, 1963. Thoughtful application of anthropological theory to the problems of the "change agent," enriched with many examples and short case histories.

Hambidge, Gove, ed., *Dynamics of Development*. New York: Praeger, 1964. A series of short articles originally published in *International Development Review*, summarizing much of the folk-wisdom of professional practitioners and scholars of development.

Hanson, John W. and Cole S. Brembeck, *Education and the Development of Nations*. New York: Holt, 1966. Some of the shorter classics dealing with the relationships between education and development, in its broadest sense, with useful bibliographic suggestions, tied together with somewhat simplistic editorial comments.

Harbison, Frederick and Charles A. Meyers, *Education, Manpower and Economic Growth: Strategies of Human Resource Development*. New York: McGraw-Hill, 1964. Good comprehensive statement of educational planning for human resource development.

Heady, Ferrel, *Public Administration: A Comparative Perspective*. Englewood Cliffs, N. J.: Prentice-Hall, 1966. Good comprehensive introductory treatment of an underdeveloped subject.

Higgins, Benjamin, *United Nations and U. S. Foreign Economic Policy*. Homewood, Illinois: Irwin, 1962. Thoughtful comparison of U.S. and UN capital and technical assistance, emerging with recommendations for finding more ways of using multilateral mechanisms.

Hirschman, Albert O., *Journeys Toward Progress: Studies in Economic Policy-Making in Latin America.* New York: Twentieth Century Fund, 1963. Valuable analysis of the processes of problem-solving in land reform, inflation, and regional development, as they unfolded in three Latin American countries, with some general advice to "reform-mongers."

——, *The Strategy of Economic Development.* New Haven: Yale University, 1958. The classic statement of the argument for "unbalanced growth" as a source of development, and of the role of foreign aid in inducing and relieving economic pressures.

Hovey, Harold A., *United States Military Assistance: A Study of Policies and Practices.* New York: Praeger, 1965. A precise, useful rehearsal of the facts, figures, and history of military aid programs, drawn largely from official but sometimes hard-to-find sources.

Industrial Council for Social and Economic Studies, *The Swedish Economy and the Underdeveloped Countries.* The Council, Skoldungagatan 2, Stockholm, O., 1961.

International Bank for Reconstruction and Development, Economic Dept., *Economic Growth and External Debt.* Baltimore, Johns Hopkins, 1964.

International Conference on Science in the Advancement of New States, 1960, *Science and the New Nations.* New York: Basic Books, 1961.

Jordan, Amos A., *Foreign Aid and the Defense of Southeast Asia.* New York: Praeger, 1962. Useful analysis of aid activities in seven "defense-support" countries in South and Southeast Asia.

Krause, W., *Economic Development: The Underdeveloped World and the American Interest.* Belmont, Cal.: Wadsworth, 1961. Good summary of the economics of development viewed in terms of foreign aid operations, reflecting needs that stem from the Eisenhower administration and have still not been fully met.

Kreinin, Mordechai E., *Israel and Africa, A Study in Technical Cooperation.* New York: Praeger, 1964. A brief sympathetic account of Israel's technical assistance to Africa and Asia, describing the advantages derived from Israel's neutrality, size, and recent emergence from dependence on foreign aid. Assistance projects in agriculture and other areas are described as well as the extensive program of training students from LDC's.

Kriesberg, Martin, ed., *Public Administration in Developing Countries.* Washington, D. C.: Brookings Institution, 1965.

Lerner, Daniel, *Passing of Traditional Society.* New York: Free Press, 1958. Pathbreaking comparative study of the sequence of social modernization, with special attention to the role of communications media.

Liska, George, *The New Statecraft: Foreign Aid in American Foreign Policy.* Chicago: University of Chicago, 1960. Good theoretical introduction to the concepts of foreign aid as an instrument of national policy.

Little, I.M.D., *Aid to Africa, An Appraisal of U.K. Policy for Aid to Africa South of the Sahara.* Oxford: Pergamon Press; New York: Macmillan, 1964. Examination of British policies and operations, with recommendations for changes that would more closely resemble American practice.

Loeber, Thomas S., *Foreign Aid: Our Tragic Experiment.* New York: Norton, 1961. Describes corruption and mismanagement as reported in audits and observed by a former ICA employee in the Middle East, presenting a series of recommendations, many of which were accepted during the Kennedy administration.

Maddison, Angus, *Foreign Skills and Technical Assistance in Economic Development.* Paris: Development Center of OECD, 1965.

Manger, William, ed., *The Alliance for Progress, A Critical Appraisal.* Washington: Public Affairs Press, 1963.

Maritano, Nino and Antonio H. Obaid, *An Alliance for Progress: Challenge and the Problem.* Minneapolis: Dennison, 1964. Presents some Latin American developmental problems and viewpoints on U.S. foreign economic policies in lively popular language.

Mason, Edward S., *Foreign Aid and Foreign Policy.* New York: Harper, 1964. The Elihu Root Lectures at the Council on Foreign Relations in May, 1963. Especially interesting for its clear analysis of the "burden-sharing" problem, the semantics of "real" aid, and the rationale of the Alliance for Progress.

McClelland, David C., *The Achieving Society*. Princeton: Van Nostrand, 1961. Significant empirical studies of motivation as a basis for change, with special attention to a sensed "need for achievement."

Mihaly, Eugene Bramer, *Foreign Aid and Politics in Nepal*. London: Oxford University, 1965. Very good case study of a variety of aid operations in a difficult and inaccessible part of the world.

Mikesell, Raymond Fred, *U. S. Private and Government Investment Abroad*. Eugene: University of Oregon, 1962. Description and history of American foreign investments, devoting some attention to their impact on the host country and offering recommendations for capital aid policy and administration.

Millikan, Max F. and W. W. Rostow, *A Proposal: Key to an Effective Foreign Policy*. New York: Harper, 1957. Pioneering venture in the effort to relate economic development aid to basic political interests of the U. S., with a fresh optimism about the prospects of contributing to a stable, democratic world order.

Montgomery, John D., *Aid to Africa: New Test for U. S. Policy*. New York: Foreign Policy Association Headline Series, No. 149, 1961. Brief introduction to the structure of foreign aid, the special problems of tropical Africa, and the coming of U.S. aid to Liberia, Ethiopia, Ghana, Guinea, and the "Junior Partnership" programs.

————, *The Politics of Foreign Aid: American Experience in Southeast Asia*. New York: Praeger, 1962. An examination of foreign aid in the context of international politics and the domestic politics of giving and receiving countries, with illustrations drawn from Taiwan, Thailand, Burma, Vietnam, Laos, and Cambodia.

————, and William J. Siffin, eds., *Approaches to Development: Politics, Administration and Change*. New York: McGraw-Hill, 1966. Chapters by Ralph Braibanti and David S. Brown explore the philosophy and experience of Americans offering technical assistance in public administration.

Moomaw, I. W., *The Challenge of Hunger, A Program for More Effective Foreign Aid*. New York: Praeger, 1966. Enthusiastic grass-roots view of the achievements and potentials of foreign aid, proposing a new semipublic institution to carry on foreign aid in order to provide continuity and improve administration.

Morley, Lorna and Felix Morley, *The Patchwork History of Foreign Aid*. Washington, D. C.: American Enterprise Association, 1961. Based on a patchwork of historical evidence, a plea for reduction of aid in order to improve the U.S. balance of payments position.

Morris, James, *The Road to Huddersfield, A Journey to Five Continents*. New York: Random House, 1963. Good journalistic survey of World Bank approaches and activities in the days of Eugene Black, complete with impressionistic reports of visits to IBRD projects in Ethiopia, Thailand, Italy, Colombia, and India.

Mosher, Arthur T., *Technical Cooperation in Latin American Agriculture*. Chicago: University of Chicago, 1957. Perceptive study of technical assistance operations, drawn from experiences in eight Latin American agricultural projects. Case studies offer both analysis and policy and operational conclusions.

Moyes, A. and T. Hayter, *World III*. New York: Pergamon, 1964.

Nwogugu, E. I., *The Legal Problems of Foreign Investment in Developing Countries*. New York: Manchester University, 1965.

Opler, Morris E., *Social Aspects of Technical Assistance in Operation*. Paris: UNESCO, 1954.

Overseas Development Institute, *Colonial Development*, 1960; *Development Guide*, 1963; *Education Assistance*, 1960; *Technical Assistance*, 1963. All three published in London, by the institute.

Owen, Wilfred, *Strategy for Mobility*. Washington, D. C.: Brookings Institution, 1964. Clear and thoughtful examination of the relationship between transportation and development with useful parallels between early American experiences and those in presently underdeveloped countries.

Paddock, William and Paul Paddock, *Hungry Nations*. Boston: Atlantic-Little, Brown, 1964. Common-sense generalizations about development, supplemented with firmly written generalizations about foreign aid; provocative, sometimes oversimplified, occasionally erroneous, but seldom dull.

Paul, Benjamin D. and Walter B. Miller, eds., *Health, Culture and Community*.

New York: Russell Sage Foundation, 1955. Extensive and useful case histories of public health projects in a wide variety of settings, usually in underdeveloped countries, supplemented by perceptive editorial comments.

Pincus, John, *Economic Aid and International Cost Sharing*. Baltimore: Johns Hopkins, 1965. Very good economic analysis of the possibility of discovering equitable means of sharing the "burden" of offering aid to underdeveloped countries.

President's Committee to Study the U.S. Military Assistance Program, *Composite Report and Annexes*. 2 vols. Washington, D. C.: Government Printing Office, 1959. Known as the "Draper Report," good source of data and authoritative interpretations of relationship of aid to national security.

Pye, Lucian, *Aspects of Political Development: An Analytic Study*. Boston: Atlantic-Little Brown, 1966. Most readable introduction to this complex subject, with many policy overtones.

Randall, Laura, ed., *Economic Development: Evolution in Revolution*. Boston: Heath, 1964. Short reader presenting reprints of significant essays on the possibility and speed of economic development.

Ranis, Gustav, ed., *The U. S. and the Developing Economies*. New York: Norton, 1964. Well-chosen essays on economics of development and foreign aid reprinted from various sources.

Rao, V.K.R.V. and Dharm Narain, *Foreign Aid and India's Economic Development*. New York: Asia Publishing House, 1963. Comprehensive survey of the amounts and kinds of aid received by India during the first and second plans, with a chapter on impact and one on problems of aid, theory, and administration in India.

Rauschenbush, Stephen, *The Challenge to the Alliance for Progress*. New York: Public Affairs Institute, 1962.

Riggs, Fred W., *Administration in Developing Countries*. Boston: Houghton Mifflin, 1964. Important contribution to the literature of comparative development, joining empirical data to theoretical analysis.

Robock, S. H., *Brazil's Developing Northeast: A Study of Regional Planning and Foreign Aid*. Washington, D. C.: Brookings Institution, 1963. Useful case study of development planning and activities in a vast region of Brazil, with many insights into the role and influence of various foreign aid instruments.

Rubin, Jacob A., *Your Hundred Billion Dollars*. Philadelphia: Chilton, 1964.

Schramm, Wilbur, *Mass Media and National Development, The Role of Information in the Developing Countries*. Stanford: Stanford University, 1964. A distinguished scholar of communications explains use of mass media as a means to development, influencing attitudes and diffusing knowledge.

Scigliano, Robert and Guy H. Fox, *Technical Assistance in Vietnam. The Michigan State University Experience*. New York: Praeger, 1965. Short case study of a large university advisory project in public and police administration.

Sharp, Walter R., *Field Administration in the UN System*. London: Stevens, 1961; New York: Praeger, 1961. Comprehensive description of administrative mechanisms of the UN involved in economic and social programs.

Shonfield, Andrew, *The Attack on World Poverty*. New York: Random House, 1960. Optimistic and still relevant appraisal of foreign aid as an alternative option to choosing the communist path to economic development. Contains succinct descriptions of bilateral, UN, and World Bank operations and limitations and offers suggestions for improvement.

Singer, Hans W., *International Development: Growth and Change*. New York: McGraw-Hill, 1964. Examination of changes in economic theories of development and the role of capital assistance. Sections deal with Africa and Northeast Brazil. Presented in popular language.

Sperling, J. Bodo, *Die Rourkela-Deutschen*. Stuttgart: Deutsche Verlags-Anstalt, 1965. Discussion of the German-Indian relationships and attitudes during construction of a large steel mill in India, by a participant in the aid project. Devotes special attention to problems of personnel and contract management.

Spicer, Edward H., ed., *Human Problems in Technological Change. A Case Book*. New York: Russell Sage Foundation, 1952. Case studies showing communities undergoing various forms of "modernization," written by eminent anthropologists. arranged and presented for instructional purposes.

Sufrin, Sidney C., *Unions in Emerging Societies, Frustration and Politics*. Syracuse: Syracuse University, 1964.

Taylor, D., *Development Means People*. New York: Pergamon, 1964.

Teaf, Howard M., Jr., and Peter G. Franck, *Hands Across Frontiers: Case Studies in Technical Cooperation.* Ithaca: Cornell University, 1955. Cases describing technical assistance projects of various types in Afghanistan, India, Taiwan, Brazil, Peru, Ceylon, Saudi Arabia, Turkey, Japan, Nigeria, and the Arab refugee settlement.

Thornton, T. P., *The Third World in Soviet Perspective.* Princeton: Princeton University, 1964. Articles by Soviet scholars, supplemented by helpful editorial comments.

Tickner, F. J., *Technical Cooperation.* New York: Hillary, 1965.

Tully, Andrew, and Milton Britten, *Where Did Your Money Go?* New York: Simon & Schuster, 1964. Journalistic exposé of waste in foreign aid.

U. S. Senate Special Committee to Study the Foreign Aid Program, *Foreign Aid Programs: Compilation of Studies and Surveys.* Washington, D. C.: Government Printing Office, 1957. Important documents prepared in the first large-scale review of early foreign aid policies and operations, including path-breaking studies by MIT and Brookings Institution.

Van der Beugel, Ernst H., *From Marshall Aid to Atlantic Partnership.* New York: Elsevier, 1966.

Walterhouse, Harry F., *A Time to Build: Military Civic Action, Medium for Economic Development and Social Reform.* Columbia: University of South Carolina, 1964. Brief case studies of military contributions to modernization, as they relate to the doctrines of "civic action."

Warne, William E., *Mission for Peace: Point Four in Iran.* Indianapolis: Bobbs-Merrill, 1956. Memoirs of a U.S. foreign aid mission director, presented in a succession of naïve anecdotes.

Waterston, Albert, *Development Planning: Lessons of Experience.* Baltimore: Johns Hopkins, 1965. Valuable practical summary of some World Bank experiences.

Weaver, James H., *The International Development Association, A New Approach to Foreign Aid.* New York: Praeger, 1965. Historical account of the establishment of the "soft loan" agency of the World Bank, larded with arguments against reliance on aid policies of exclusively hard loans or bilateral arrangements.

Weidner, Edward W., *Technical Assistance in Public Administration Overseas: The Case for Development Administration.* Chicago: Public Administration Service, 1964. Useful, comprehensive reference work on efforts to improve developmental capabilities overseas through technical assistance.

Westwood, Andrew F., *Foreign Aid in a Foreign Policy Framework.* Washington, D. C.: Brookings Institution, 1966. Short, basic, useful policy history of U.S. involvement in foreign aid.

Whitman, M. von N., *Government Risk-Sharing in Foreign Investment.* Princeton: Princeton University, 1965.

Wiggins, J. W. and Helmut Schoeck, eds., *Foreign Aid Reexamined—A Critical Appraisal.* Washington, D. C.: Public Affairs Press, 1958. A series of strongly, sometimes harshly critical views on the impact and the potentials of U.S. foreign aid.

Witt, Lawrence and Carl Eicher, *The Effects of U. S. Agricultural Surplus Disposal Programs on Recipient Countries.* East Lansing: Michigan State University Dept. of Agricultural Economics, 1964. Valuable economic analysis of the problems of substituting commodities for dollars in offering aid.

Wolf, Charles, *Foreign Aid: Theory and Practice in Southern Asia.* Princeton: Princeton University, 1960. Careful examination of the history of U.S. and Soviet economic and military aid to South and Southeast Asia with view to developing a theory for the rational allocation of funds in terms of long-range purposes.

Woodbridge, George, *UNRRA: History of UN Relief and Rehabilitation Administration.* New York: Columbia University, 1950. 3 vols. Definitive history of the first large-scale international foreign aid operations.

Worsley, Peter, *The Third World.* Chicago: University of Chicago, 1965.

Zack, Arnold, *Labor Training in Developing Countries, A Challenge in Responsible Democracy.* New York: Praeger, 1964. Labor leadership training in nine centers in the underdeveloped world is examined as a contribution to economic and political development.

Index